THE THEATRE GUILD

THE FIRST TEN YEARS

By Walter Prichard Eaton

WITH ARTICLES BY
The Directors

Upsala College
Library
East Orange, N. J. 07019

New York · BRENTANO'S · *Mcmxxix*

Republished 1971
Scholarly Press, 22929 Industrial Drive East
St. Clair Shores, Michigan 48080

792.0973
E14t

Library of Congress Catalog Card Number: 71-144995
Standard Book Number 403-00922-7

167825

FOREWORD

This book is a record of the activities of the Theatre Guild during its first ten years. Mr. Eaton has acted in the role of historian, and we thank him for his generosity towards our faults. We have always wished our work to speak for itself, and are still reluctant to speak about it ourselves. The chapters which we of the Guild's directorate have contributed are based upon our actual experiences with the Guild, and are offered in the sincere belief that these experiences may be helpful to others interested in the art of the theatre.

It is not the province of this book to record our own estimate of those who have assisted us in our work. It is clear, however, that, whatever may have been the value of our own contribution, our work would have gone for nothing had we been unable to secure the coöperation of distinguished actors and actresses. These, fortunately for us, came forward and joined with us from our earliest days, often at a sacrifice to themselves. To them, our collaborators, who have made our efforts possible, we tender our affectionate appreciation. We cannot neglect the opportunity which this book affords to recite the names of the members of our present Acting Company and

Foreword

former players to whom we owe our special thanks and gratitude:

To Alfred Lunt, who has portrayed twelve characters in Guild plays, and especially for his performances in "The Guardsman," "Arms and the Man," "Ned McCobb's Daughter," "The Brothers Karamazov," "Juarez and Maximilian," "The Second Man," "The Doctor's Dilemma" and as *Mosca* in "Volpone;" to Lynn Fontanne, who has appeared in nine Guild plays, and notably in "The Guardsman," "Arms and the Man," "At Mrs. Beam's," "The Doctor's Dilemma," "Caprice," as *Liza* in "Pygmalion" and as *Nina Leeds* in "Strange Interlude;" Dudley Digges, veteran of fourteen plays, especially remembered in the roles of *Jimmy Caesar* in "John Ferguson," of *Clegg* in "Jane Clegg," of *The Sparrow* in "Liliom," of *Mr. Zero* in "The Adding Machine," of *Volpone*, and of *Undershaft* in "Major Barbara;" Helen Westley who (though she thanks herself, a not altogether un-Westley-ian gesture) has appeared in thirty-eight Guild productions, conspicuous among them "Jane Clegg," "Liliom," "He Who Gets Slapped," "The Adding Machine," "Fata Morgana," "Volpone," "The Guardsman" and "The Camel Through the Needle's Eye;" Henry Travers, beloved character actor of the Guild, who has played no less than twenty roles, notably *Mr. Munce* in "Jane Clegg," *The Burglar* in "Heartbreak House," *Alfred Doolittle* in "Pygmalion," *Corbaccio* in "Volpone" and *Pesta* in "The Camel Through the Needle's

Foreword

Eye;" Ernest Cossart, who has appeared in seven Guild roles, among them *Briquet* in "He Who Gets Slapped," *Corbino* in "Volpone" and *B. B.* in "The Doctor's Dilemma;" and to Margalo Gillmore for her performances in "He Who Gets Slapped," "The Silver Cord," "Marco Millions" and "The Second Man."

To Earle Larimore who has appeared in five Guild plays and whose performances in "The Silver Cord," "The Second Man" and "Strange Interlude" are especially noteworthy; to Glenn Anders for his excellent work in "They Knew What They Wanted," "Strange Interlude" and "Dynamo;" Tom Powers for his portrayal of *Charlie* in "Strange Interlude;" Eliot Cabot, whose performances in "The Silver Cord," "Major Barbara" and "The Camel Through the Needle's Eye" are gratefully remembered; Elizabeth Risdon, for her work in "Heartbreak House" and "The Silver Cord;" George Gaul, remembered in "Back to Methuselah," "The Brothers Karamazov" and "Faust;" Morris Carnovsky and Philip Leigh, veterans of many Guild productions; Alexander Kirkland and Frank Conroy for their fine work in "Wings Over Europe;" to Douglass Montgomery, Claude Rains and Gale Sondergaard, present members, and to Clare Eames, Edward G. Robinson and Philip Loeb, former members of the Acting Company.

Space does not permit of our mentioning all of the other players whose fine performances have contributed to the Guild's success but we cannot refrain from citing a certain

Foreword

number. Our grateful appreciation is due to Laura Hope Crews for her work in " Mr. Pim Passes By," " The Silver Cord " and other Guild plays; to Margaret Wycherley for her performances in " Jane Clegg " and " The Adding Machine;" Joseph Schildkraut for his *Liliom* and *Peer Gynt*; Eva Le Gallienne for her *Julie* in " Liliom;" Richard Bennett for his performances in " He Who Gets Slapped " and " They Knew What They Wanted;" Frank Reicher for his *Mancini* in the same play and *The Cashier* in " From Morn to Midnight;" Winifred Lenihan for her *St. Joan*; Ben Ami for his performance in " The Failures;" Emily Stevens for her work in " Fata Morgana;" Pauline Lord for her *Amy* in " They Knew What They Wanted;" to Blanche Yurka for her work in " Man and the Masses;" June Walker for " Processional " and " The Glass Slipper;" Helen Hayes for her *Cleopatra*; and to Jean Cadell for her performance in " At Mrs. Beam's."

To Rollo Peters, Augustin Duncan, Erskine Sanford, Effie Shannon, Lucille Watson, Hortense Alden, Florence Eldridge, Dennis King, Phyllis Povah, Celia Adler, Louis Calvert, and many others who helped toward the success of our first few years.

For their admirable playing of one or more leading parts, we are indebted to Judith Anderson, George Abbott, Estelle Winwood, Balliol Holloway, Basil Sidney, Roland Young, Arnold Daly, Kenneth MacKenna, Percy Waram, Frieda Inescort, Donald MacDonald, Ernest Lawford, Lionel Atwill, McKay Morris, Helen Chandler, Claudette

Foreword

Colbert, Miriam Hopkins, Albert Bruning, Morgan Farley, Lee Baker, José Ruben, Reginald Mason, and to Rose MacClendon, Frank Wilson, Jack Carter, Georgette Harvey, Evelyn Ellis and the other excellent members of the "Porgy" cast who have played so long and so faithfully in that play.

We regret that lack of space forbids the mention of the many others whose work in both large and small parts has been of tremendous value to the Guild. To them, also, our sincerest appreciation.

THE DIRECTORS

CONTENTS

THE HISTORY OF THE THEATRE GUILD
By Walter Prichard Eaton

PAGE 3

BEHIND THE SCENES WITH THE EXECUTIVE DIRECTOR
By Theresa Helburn

PAGE 128

THE GUILD AND PRODUCTION
By Philip Moeller

PAGE 154

AN ART THEATRE WITHOUT ENDOWMENT
By Maurice Wertheim

PAGE 170

Contents

THE ACTOR'S RELATION TO THE ART THEATRE AND VICE VERSA
By Helen Westley

PAGE 179

SETTING THE STAGE
By Lee Simonson

PAGE 184

THE LITTLE THEATRE GROWS UP
By Lawrence Langner

PAGE 207

CASTS OF THE THEATRE GUILD SUBSCRIPTION PRODUCTIONS

PAGE 231

THE THEATRE GUILD

THE FIRST TEN YEARS

THE HISTORY OF THE THEATRE GUILD

By Walter Prichard Eaton

I

The Cast

On April 10, 1929, the Theatre Guild of New York celebrated its tenth birthday. In a single decade this organization has grown from an extremely humble and, indeed, semi-amateur beginning to the undisputed leadership of the American theatre. It has become, in fact, one of the foremost producing organizations of the world, if we take into consideration its standard of plays, its skill in presentation, and the extent of territory and population which it now serves. Beginning in the tiny Garrick Theatre on West 35th Street, New York (a theatre built originally by Harrigan and Hart, and once conducted by Richard Mansfield), with audiences even smaller than the seating capacity of the house, the Guild goes into its eleventh year the owner of its own theatre in New York, and the lessee of two others; it has more than 30,000 season subscribers to its New York productions, and an equal number of subscribers divided among six other cities, where it showed its company in 1928–29. It will, in its eleventh year, add three more cities to its subscription circuit, send a repertoire company on tour of the smaller places, and continue the tour of " Strange Interlude." It has even invaded London with " Porgy " and " Caprice."

But all this would be but another boast of size, and of no real consequence, were it not for the remarkable fact that the Guild plays are for the most part the antithesis of the type of drama supposedly popular and able to succeed on tour; they are for the most part plays with a sharp intellectual appeal, or with some edge of wit or style or sophistication setting them off from the ruck. At times they are experimental in construction or production — though not as often as some people could wish. Chiefly, however, they are differentiated by some " spire of meaning " (in Galsworthy's phrase), some intellectual appeal, which makes their success the more surprising, and gives, of course, to the Guild its chief banner of leadership.

What is behind this organization to bring about such results? Why is it that a group of young people in 1919 — nearly all of them amateurs of the theatre — could start a playhouse which has grown to dominate our stage? What has kept this group so uniformly successful, and so healthily expanding year by year, growing as a tree grows, deepening its roots and spreading its branches? The answer to that question is vital, and gives meaning to the story that follows.

The Theatre Guild consists of six men and women, all but two of them members of the Board from its inception, and those other two members from very early days. It is less a theatre of ideas than of an idea. That idea is shared by these six men and women, and by each one is held with passionate loyalty. It is not a new idea, except as the Guild has worked it out in practical detail. It has been held by many a lone artist of the theatre in times past; it animated the founders of the Moscow Art Theatre, it was inculcated in several of the Guild directors by teachers in their universities. But it came into the American playhouse of commerce, a playhouse sadly disrupted and abased by two decades of commercial warfare, by " syndicates " and ignorant shopkeeping, at a time when it was sorely needed and had all the force of revolution; and it was held not by a lone artist, but by six men and women of vision and persistence who could stand together for mutual help.

And what is that idea? Ridiculously simple! Merely that the theatre is bigger than any workers in it, and in its ideal condition will not be employed for either personal or commercial exploitation, but for the creation, as carefully and lovingly as lies within one's power, of the best drama of one's time, drama honestly reflecting the author's vision of life or sense of style and beauty. This idea, if it is sincerely held, carries as corollary the belief that in their hearts many theatregoers must also prefer it to any lower standard. The founders of the Theatre Guild believed that. If they hadn't, they would not have founded the Guild. And, of course, they were right.

I say this idea, brought into our playhouse by the Guild, had the force of revolution. This is why: our playhouse, save in lone and struggling instances, had existed as a business, and for the exploitation of its artists. It was as if somebody should set up a school to capitalize his teaching ability, which might be genuine and great, but the school, of course, would perish with his passing. The Guild founded a university. This figure is not so far fetched as it may seem. The parallel between the Guild and a university is closer, perhaps, than any other you could devise for illustration. In a faculty meeting of a university many and divergent views are expressed, opinions clash, discussion may even become heated, but in the end what happens? Every member is working for the lasting good of education and the usefulness of his college, and the final vote represents — ideally, at any rate — not personal desires but a belief in how best to attain to an ideal goal. It represents loyalty to an idea. So in the Theatre Guild the six directors, flying directly in the face of the dictum that the theatre must always have a " czar," do nothing except as a whole. They pick the plays to produce, they determine policies, they even guide the actual staging of the play, by meeting and vote of the whole Board. They early adopted and strictly have adhered to a rule that no member's own work shall be exploited, and the devotion of the six is concentrated on selecting and producing the works of others. To what end? To the ideal end that the theatre they have created shall be the best possible theatre, not a theatre of commerce, but a theatre for the flowering of true dramatic art; though, quite unlike a university, this theatre is self-supporting. Just as loyalty to the idea of a university unifies and dignifies the debates of a faculty, loyalty to this idea of a theatre unifies and dignifies the weekly " soviets " of the Theatre Guild directors.

One of the directors may like a play hugely, but unless he can persuade the rest that it fits into their group idea of a theatre, they will never produce it. Six points of view may be clashing, over a play, the choice of an actor, the wisdom of a road tour, what not; they may be clashing with a good deal of apparent acidulousness, and hopelessly at variance. But what brings, at last, the harmony of a decision is precisely what brings it to a debating faculty — the guiding loyalty to an idea bigger and more enduring than an individual or his opinions; in this case, the idea of a theatre dedicated to enduring dramatic art. Without that loyalty, shared by all and passionately held by each, the directors of the Theatre Guild would never have assembled in the first place, and could never have stood together and accomplished what they have in these last ten years.

The production methods, the business methods, of the Guild are interesting, and deserve careful attention. But no other groups can hope to do similar work if they fail to grasp this underlying secret of the Guild's success — loyalty, above all personal considerations of every sort, to the idea of the enduring theatre, and willingness to sacrifice all personal interests and hobbies, if need be, to this idea as it crystallizes in the group.

Who are the six who constitute this revolutionary theatrical soviet? The most striking feature about them, no doubt, is their academic background, their approach to the playhouse through the new channels which have been ploughed only in this century.

Miss Helen Westley, to be sure, was a professional actress before the organization of the Guild, or of its fumbling predecessor, the Washington Square Players, with which she was also connected. She is, however, a graduate of the American Academy of Dramatic Arts and the Emerson School of Oratory in Boston, which was a pioneer a generation and more ago in the then dubious experiment of linking education with theatre practice. Besides her special gifts as an actress, Miss Westley contributed to the organization an original personality, with a mind more than unusually free from social or conventional prejudices. Her catholicity of taste in the selection of plays, and her uncompromising devotion to the ideals of the art theatre have made her a collaborator whose sincerity has always been respected by her associates, even when there have been wide variations of opinion between her and them on matters of policy and play selection.

Miss Theresa Helburn, whose official post in the Guild is

that of Executive Director, and who joined the Board in its second year, having previously been their play reader, is a graduate of Bryn Mawr and a student of Professor George P. Baker's "English 47," in which she worked as a graduate student at Radcliffe. Before her connection with the Guild, she had written several plays, had two professional productions and spent a season writing dramatic criticism for the "Nation." Neither the necessity for a livelihood, nor the accident of environment, nor exhibitionism, drew her into the playhouse, but rather that new and idealistic enthusiasm for the theatre as an art so characteristic of the academic and amateur movement which began in the first decade of this century. Fitted by temperament and training for a comprehension of the artistic problems of the Guild, Miss Helburn has adapted herself with great resourcefulness to the difficult duties of executive director. Here her capacity for clear objective thinking has stood the Guild organization in good stead throughout the many tangled problems of organization, and her discerning taste has been of the greatest advantage in the selection of plays. Moreover, Miss Helburn's talents in the casting of plays has been marked.

Philip Moeller's special contribution to the group achievement has been chiefly as a director, for which he early developed unusual aptitude. He is a graduate of Columbia. So fond was he of academic life that he remained under the tutelage of Brander Matthews and others from 1901 to 1908, but found no subsequent outlet for his theatrical interest, save in amateur work, until he helped to start the Washington Square Players, and wrote for them several one-act skits (such as the now famous "Helena's Husbands"), which he himself directed. Several plays from his pen, acted by Henry Miller, Mrs. Fiske, and others followed. But his playwrighting has been put aside since the formation of the Guild. To the Guild idea, which precludes the exploitation of member work, he has subordinated his personal ambitions as an author, in order to carry out, as stage director, the group ideals of production. While Mr. Moeller has made the greater number of successful productions for the Guild, the impression of his personality upon the work of the Guild does not end upon the stage. Endowed with a sensitively aesthetic imagination, his talents have been equally employed in the selection of the Guild plays and the actors who play in them. His buoyant enthusiasms have carried the Guild Board over many a difficult artistic obstacle, and his contribution has been as varied and imaginative as his own exuberant personality.

Lee Simonson's chief contribution to the Guild has been, of course, as a scene designer and technical expert. But he did not come into the group from any "scenic studio." He is a graduate of Harvard, attended "English 47" and is one of a brilliant crowd of young men who emerged from Harvard in the earlier years of the century, almost bumptious with creative zest. Simonson and Robert Edmond Jones were both painters whom a new spirit in our theatre

The First Ten Years

called into the playhouse. Simonson continues many interests outside the theatre, having edited "Creative Art," designed furniture and interiors, and the like. But it was his theatre study at Harvard which gave him, of course, his first understanding of the new possibilities of graphic creation in alliance with the drama, and it was the Washington Square Players which gave him his first practical opportunity to practice and experiment. He came into the Guild at its inception as a technical expert in design, but self-taught under a new theatrical regime, and in full understanding of the group idea of theatrical art. But like all other directors of the Guild, Simonson's contribution is not one-sided. His very definite ideas upon the Guild policies, his mental honesty and his wide cultural interests have been brought to bear upon every problem of the Guild, both from the artistic and the organization standpoint. Equipped with an analytical mind, which is unusual in the artist, Simonson's attitude about all Guild problems is characterized by a thoroughness and a determination to get at the bottom of things which has been of the greatest value to his colleagues.

The remaining two directors divide their interest in the Guild with other occupations. Lawrence Langner (the only foreign-born member of the group) is a member of an International Patent law firm and a playwright, and Maurice Wertheim is a banker. It is probable that their connection with other and so diverse pursuits is a great asset to the Guild, causing them to bring

The Theatre Guild

an unjaded enthusiasm and a fresh point of view to its deliberations.

Mr. Langner, one of the founders of the Guild, as he was of the preceding Washington Square Players, was born in England, early developed a fondness for the theatre, and coming to New York to make his home joined with various amateurs in Greenwich Village in reading or producing member work. He, too, had aspirations toward authorship; the Washington Square Players produced various of his one-act plays and managers other than the Guild have more recently produced longer works of his. His play, "Moses," has been published, though not produced. But he, like the rest, subordinated any personal ambition to the group idea in the Guild activities. Perhaps Langner's greatest contribution to the Guild idea was his foresight in organization. As he was the progenitor of the Guild, his attitude has always been that of an anxious parent, looking out for the future of his offspring. While others were contending with immediate and pressing exigencies, Langner was envisaging problems far in the future and devising means of settling them in advance. He has always, so to speak, discounted the Guild's artistic notes before they came due. He it was, for example, who worried the other directors into a realization of the necessity of having their own playhouse years before that need became a fact, and he it was who kept urging the impossibility of ever achieving even a modified repertory without an acting company. Whatever emergencies had to be met, Langner was always ready to sacrifice all other claims to help meet them. In the large family of his interests, the Guild is undoubtedly the "white-headed boy."

Mr. Wertheim also is a graduate of Harvard and of Professor Baker's courses there, having been a member of "English 47" the first year it was given. But with him there was probably not even a lurking idea that he would enter the theatre professionally. His future as a banker was foreordained. Consequently, following his graduation, he had little or no outlet for his theatrical enthusiasms and love for the creative life of the theatre, until he allied himself with the Washington Square Players, which resulted in his later connection with the Guild. To their deliberations, he brought not only his business wisdom, sorely needed of course in those first years of trial, but all his tastes and enthusiasms which heretofore had had no opportunity for expression. Here he could argue and plead to make them prevail. He could help in the choice of plays and in the essential work of keeping them going. He could put behind the work of the Guild his resourcefulness and the drive of his dynamic personality. He could project his conception that a theatre which was not self-supporting would lose vital touch with the public, and could not be permanent, so that not only for its ultimate freedom and self-respect, but for its best service to the art of the theatre in general, the Guild should never seek an endowment, but always pay its own way — one of the fundamental policies of the organization.

Thus, to the group idea, each of the six members of the Guild has brought his or her contribution, and merged it in the general whole, nor has each contribution necessarily been of technical skill in actual creation. But it has always been something vitally concerned with the idea of a theatre bigger than its workers, and it has been freely given, in a spirit of complete loyalty and devotion to this idea. In this book, each director will tell, in his or her own way, as no outsider, of course, can, something of the particular ideas and impulses behind the individual contributions. But modesty, or our latter-day fear of any expression of personal idealism, may perhaps keep them from sufficiently indicating the fact that at bottom it was the devotion of each to the idea of enduring dramatic art, devotion great enough to sink all personal ambitions in the general good and to make the Guild for all of them a lifelong outlet for their creative powers at their best and most unselfish pitch, which carried this organization through to success and has won for it the enthusiastic confidence of America.

II

The Backgrounds

THE progress of the American theatre, and still more perhaps of the American drama, has been more than once delayed or even set back by forces larger than the theatre, or forces in the theatre acting in an unpredictable fashion. It is a fact we are coming to recognize, that in the middle years of the last century our stage was healthily alive with native entertainments, particularly minstrel shows and clever burlesques, which were rapidly breaking down the pseudo-classic tradition and laying the necessary ground work for a modern drama. Our actors especially were keenly observant of contemporary life, and there were not wanting foreign visitors in those days who found in our theatre a vitality lacking in England. Then came the Civil War.

The Civil War not only had the direct and quite predictable effect of taking men's minds away from the relatively trivial affairs of art and creating an aftermath of weariness and laxity, during which on the stage "leg shows" flourished at times almost to the exclusion of other entertainment; but it had the unpredictable effect of greatly expanding the country westward and creating many towns capable of supporting a theatre, but without any local stock company rooted in a tradition and trained to present a varied fare. Led by Dion Boucicault, who as early as 1861 had organized a special company to take one of his plays on tour, managers began to cast plays in New York and send them around the country, scenery and all, as rivals to the older stock companies, or as substitutes for them. Quite naturally these companies took out plays which were thought most likely to be widely popular, for there was now the chance of a large financial return from a successful production. Local companies and audiences, which had before the War been working together to evolve indigenous entertainment (such as Chanfrau's "Mose the Fireman" in New York) were progressively submerged, as were the steadying standards which came from a changing repertoire which always included some of the classics — the real classics. There is little doubt but the Civil War set back the development of our drama and helped to create confusion in the organization of our theatre. Had it not come, it may well be that to an American rather than to Tom Robertson would have gone the credit for the first modern dramas in English.

There was at least one great compensation. Playwrighting became for the first time in America a profitable profession, by which a man could support himself exclusively, and acquired a new dignity. Those playwrights, however, who felt the influence of the new drama of Europe had a hard time. James A. Herne had himself to produce his "Margaret Flemming," in 1890, for no manager would back it. Neither, strange as it seems today, would any manager back his "Shore Acres" three years later. That play was produced by a Chicago stock company first, and without the quiet ending. Its real production, in its integrity, was made by the old Boston Museum stock company, one of the last, as it had long been one of the finest acting companies in America devoted to a wide range of drama and rooted in the traditions of a single community. Herne's pioneer experiment with "Margaret Flemming," made first in Boston, was witnessed by comparatively few people, but many of those were young writers and enthusiasts, especially from the colleges, and Herne's example led to several other experiments in the 'nineties by groups organized to produce Ibsen, Hauptmann, and other examples of the new drama. What effect it might have had on the so-called "commercial managers" we shall never know.

For before the 'nineties were over an economic development had taken place in the United States which profoundly affected the theatre. Mr. Rockefeller and others had discovered the Trust, or huge combination of an industry to bring about a monopoly, and it was probably inevitable that the business men of the theatre, who had long seen much of their profits come from road tours, but profits which had to be shared with the various theatres, should conceive the idea of themselves owning or controlling all the theatres, and thus pocketing all the profits. Accordingly, the "Theatrical Syndicate" was formed, and set about to gain control of such a chain of theatres as would make booking with them inevitable. In spite of the opposition of many managers and actors, the Syndicate succeeded in its purpose. The last of the old-time stock companies disappeared. The ambitious actor or producer who might wish to experiment or to do some fine thing limited in its appeal, either had to do it as best he could, at his own risk, and often in a poor theatre, or give it up. Of course there were exceptions. The productions of Charles Frohman, a member of the Syndicate, were often excellent, and artists like Mansfield, Mrs. Fiske, and Belasco stuck to their guns. But by and large, productions had to conform to mass taste to get a profitable hearing, much as the motion pictures do today. Without any question this was a severe setback to the development of modern American drama, and Fitch, Moody, Walter, and other dramatists who wrote in the first decade of this century accomplished what they did with no organized theatre to help them. Moody was least affected, as he was least a man of the theatre, and his producer was Henry Miller, himself an artist.

The grip of the Syndicate, after a decade, was broken, but not by any reëstablishment of local theatres; a rival chain of New York controlled houses was built, that is all. Competition in mediocrity was established. And then came the motion pictures.

The First Ten Years

Rapidly, and increasingly, the motion pictures took away from the theatre its gallery audiences, and the motion picture houses, too, could be operated in the smaller towns with greater regularity and at smaller expense. They created a sudden crisis in the playhouse which our theatre was not organized to meet. The pictures were increasing the competition in mediocrity, with the advantage of low-scale admission on their side, whereas they offered little or no competition in poetry, intellectual excitement, social criticism, and other things provided by the drama in its best estate, more particularly the modern drama as it had been developed during the previous generation, and which was at the time so enthusiastically studied in our universities and read by many people everywhere.

It was, indeed, a paradox of the times that when our professional theatre was at low ebb, our universities had begun to teach play writing and play producing, amateur enthusiasts were banding together, young artists were looking with fascination at the " new stage craft " of Europe, and there was a surge of creative life seeking some sort of an outlet in expression, an outlet the organized theatre did not provide.

Such, very briefly, was the process of development which led to the formation of the Washington Square Players in New York City, as well as the Provincetown Players, and other similar experiments. But the Washington Square Players are of peculiar interest here, as they were the direct forerunners of the Guild. They were for the most part amateurs, many of them graduates of that new university study of the theatre, all of them eager to have some hand in dramatic production and dissatisfied with the kind of dramatic production made in the commercial playhouse. It might be easy to exaggerate their interest in reform: doubtless their desire to be doing something creative themselves chiefly moved them to action. But there is no doubt of their scorn for the flabby, purposeless, and false plays then more or less compelled by conditions in the theatre and their enthusiasm for what they considered a more honest art. With the success of such foreign ventures as the Abbey Theatre and the Moscow Art Theatre in mind, they rented the little Band Box Theatre on East 57th Street, New York, early in 1915 and issued the following manifesto, which is still interesting for the light it sheds on subsequent ideals of the Guild:

"The Washington Square Players, Inc. — an organization which takes its name from the district where it originated — is composed of individuals who believe in the future of the theatre in America, and includes playwrights, actors and producers, working with a common end in view. The fact that the Drama League can recommend at the present time, as worthy of the attention of its members, only three plays running in New York City (of which two are by foreign authors, while two productions are by English and part-English companies) is an incisive comment upon the present condition of the American drama. The Washington Square Players believe that a higher standard can be reached only as the outcome of experiment and initiative. Just as the finished productions of Mr. Granville Barker, which are now delighting New York audiences at Wallack's Theatre, are the culmination of a growth of some years in the development of new methods of acting and production in English drama, so we believe that hard work and perseverance, coupled with ability and the absence of purely commercial considerations, may result in the birth and healthy growth of an artistic theatre in this country. Your whole-hearted support — a sympathetic appreciation of the possibilities of our experiment — will encourage us to greater efforts.

"We have only one policy in regard to the plays which we will produce — they must have artistic merit. Preference will be given to American plays, but we shall also include in our repertory the works of well-known European authors which have been ignored by the commercial managers.

"Though not organized for purposes of profit, we are not endowed. Money alone has never produced an artistic theatre. We are going to defray the expenses of our productions by the sale of tickets and subscriptions. Believing in democracy in the theatre, we have fixed the charge for admission at 50 cents. If we can secure sufficient support by the purchase of individual tickets, or subscriptions for ten tickets (two for each of our monthly performances) at the cost of $5.00, we shall be able to continue our work.

"If you are in sympathy with our aims, we shall welcome you in our organization. You may be able to help us in a number of ways, whether you be playwright, actor, producer, or capable of assisting us in some executive capacity.

"Our ultimate success depends upon our ability to accomplish our purpose AND your interest."

The Theatre Guild

Two things are especially to be noted in this Manifesto: first, the insistence that the Players had no set policy in the choice of plays, further than to insist on those having "artistic merit," preferring American work and giving precedence to dramas "ignored by the commercial managers"; and second, that the theatre was to be "democratic," with a 50-cent scale, and the inauguration of season subscriptions. The Theatre Guild of today has continued to choose plays on the basis of artistic value and to some extent still on their unsuitability to the needs of commercial managers, and it has based its stability on the system of season subscriptions. The "democratic" purpose of the Washington Square Players was perhaps a gesture, if unconsciously so. Probably 50 cents a seat was all they expected the traffic would bear for their experiment. The experiment, however, was democratic in a much more genuine sense. It was not superimposed from above by certain rich men. It rose spontaneously from the desires of the actual workers for a chance at self-expression, and looked for audience to men and women likeminded in discontent with the existing playhouse. Probably the desire for self-expression was a bit stronger, too, than the discontent with existing conditions! It was happy, carefree, youthful, and essentially amateur.

At first the Players planned to give but two performances a week, on Friday and Saturday evenings. The actors all volunteered their services, there being no money to pay them, and there were no newspaper advertisements for the same reason, but on February 19, 1915, the dramatic critics of New York journeyed sceptically over into the unknown regions of East 57th Street, prepared to be bored by one more exhibition of what they sometimes called the Uplift. There is nothing your New York dramatic critic is more sceptical of than the Uplift, especially when effected by amateurs. What happened was a surprise, not only to the critics, but to the friends of the Players, who constituted most of that first audience. There were three one-act plays, and a pantomime. The plays were "Licensed" by Basil Lawrence (Lawrence Langner), "Eugenically Speaking" by the director, Edward Goodman, and "Interior" by Maeterlinck. The two original plays were frank and racy without any of the offense common to Broadway attempts at frankness and raciness, and "Interior," staged with the help of Robert Edmond Jones at a cost of $35, laid a spell of suggestive visual beauty and haunting mood over the astonished house. The pantomime, "Another Interior" (originally, I believe, a college skit) showed the interior of a human stomach, into which descended various concoctions to the exceeding hurt of its hero, Gastric Juice. If memory serves us, Philip Moeller distinguished himself by his impersonation of a highly colored cordial. It wasn't an important production, though at least it was something the commercial managers would ignore; but it was merry and odd. The acting for the most part, in all the plays, was obviously amateur, even at times fumbling. Certain critics complained of this. But the zest and spirit of the productions, the hushed mood struck by the staging of "Interior," the youthful spirit of adventure which permeated the playhouse, caught everybody's fancy. The next night the theatre was sold out, and soon a third weekly performance had to be added.

On March 26, a second bill was staged, including John Reed's "Moondown" and a pretty pantomime by Holland Hudson, "The Shepherd in the Distance." The third bill was shown on May 7, which included two original plays, "April" by Rose Pastor Stokes, and "Saviors" by Edward Goodman. For their fourth bill, the Players reënacted three of their most popular productions, and added Chekhov's "The Bear."

The next autumn they reopened the Band Box on October 4, 1915, with an augmented staff of actors and other workers, and now undertook to pay these workers $25 a week, to give seven instead of three performances weekly, to pay $250 instead of $35 weekly rental, and finally to ask the public $1 instead of 50 cents for a seat. Thus does "democracy" fly out of the window when expenses come in at the door! The payment to the actors, and even the acquisition of a few trained players like Frank Conroy, didn't appear greatly to improve the standard of acting, which remained decidedly amateur. But the first bill disclosed a capital historical burlesque by Philip Moeller, "Helena's Husband," now a classic of the Little Theatres, and the second bill, which included de Musset's "Whims" (totally beyond the acting skill of the company), was notable for Alice Gerstenberg's "Overtones." This odd little comedy, which discloses two women shadowed by their "real selves," the former speaking the commonplaces of polite neutrality, the latter emitting the most outrageous honesty, oddly previsioned the technique of Eugene O'Neill's "Strange Interlude." By the time the third bill was reached, the acting had begun to improve, and with this improvement came an increase in public patronage. A critic, writing at the time, said, "Ultimately, no experimental theatre can succeed until it develops a company of players who can act. Enthusiasm, clever plays, picturesque and novel scenery, will never be a permanent substitute for acting." How true this is, the Theatre Guild was later to discover.

The third bill was most important for "The Clod," by Lewis Beach, a tabloid melodrama of the Civil War adroitly acted by Miss Josephine Meyer and rich both in theatrical suspense and spiritual suggestiveness. The fourth bill contained Zoe Akins' experiment in a free verse play about New York, "The Magical City," made interesting rather more by Lee Simonson's beautiful and imaginative setting than by Miss Akins' free verse.

On May 7, 1916, the Players gave their first long play, Maeterlinck's "Aglavaine and Selysette," a single performance for subscribers. The scenery was more notable than the acting. The last bill was Chekhov's "The Sea Gull," acted from May 22 to June 1, when the Players moved to the Comedy Theatre close to Broadway.

The Theatre Guild

It was a fine gesture on their part to close their experiment at the Band Box with "The Sea Gull," the play which made the Moscow Art Theatre famous. It was, of course, their interest in this Russian experiment which dictated the choice. But, alas! Chekhov's plays are Russian of the Russians, and a production of one of them, however well done, however interesting to the student of the contemporary theatre, could hardly strike such a chord in the public consciousness of America as to establish the group producing it as a national institution. Nor were the Washington Square Players as yet able even to give "The Sea Gull" an illuminating production. It lay a considerable distance beyond their powers. To take a single phase, in Chekhov's dramas of irresolution much of the effect is gained by sudden transitions from strong emotion of irrelevancy, and such sudden transitions are one of the severest tests of acting skill. The production, then, remained a gesture, to remind the initiate what far-off goal these young people had their gaze upon — an Art Theatre like that in Moscow!

The Players had rented the Comedy Theatre because the Band Box was too small to yield sufficient revenue to meet their rising expenses and satisfy their ambitions to employ better actors, nor could they increase their prices in a house so far from Broadway. But by coming to Broadway, they inevitably entered into competition with it; they lost much of the amateur atmosphere, the joyous playboy spirit, which had charmed people at the Band Box, and they had nothing to meet the competition with but one-act plays.

The First Ten Years

The one-act play has performed a great service to our stage. It gave the Washington Square Players, the Provincetown Players, and many a Little Theatre elsewhere, their starts. It gave practice to men like Eugene O'Neill and Paul Green. It is still the medium in scores of places for the first tentative experiments in local or folk drama. But it has never been popular in our professional theatre, except as a curtain raiser, or afterpiece, to a long play, and most people, at heart, greatly prefer a long play, even in the amateur theatre, to a bill of four one-act dramas, tolerating the latter only for special reasons. Coming, then, into direct competition with amusement seeking Broadway, at almost Broadway admission prices, the Washington Square Players were at a decided disadvantage. They found the supply of one-acters running low; it was difficult to secure original work which could meet both their literary standard and the test of Broadway popularity; they were driven back more and more on translations. But they made several worthy contributions, nonetheless, including Edward Massey's "Plots and Playwrights," and they gave Broadway hearing to O'Neill's "In the Zone," Susan Glaspell's "Trifles," and Zona Gale's "Neighbors." During their first season at the Comedy they produced, January 14, 1917, two long plays, "The Life of Man" by Andreiev, and Ibsen's "Ghosts," with Mary Shaw as a star. During their second and last season, they produced Lawrence Langner's "The Family Exit" (September 17, 1917), "Youth" by Miles Malleson (February 20, 1918) and revived "Mrs.

Warren's Profession" (March 11, 1918). This play, which on its first production by Arnold Daly in 1905 had been closed by the police, and later given a clean bill of health by the courts, was the Players' only experiment with Shaw. It did not prove profitable. Indeed, the experiment at the Comedy was no longer a success financially; quite the reverse. The World War, in which America was now actively participating, was taking its toll of the Players, and public interest was centred in more dramatic matters than plays, short or long. The last bill was staged on May 13, 1918, suggestively including Susan Glaspell's "Close the Book," and shortly thereafter the organization disbanded.

In the four years of its existence it had produced 62 one-act plays and pantomimes and 6 long dramas. Of these 68 plays, 38 were of American authorship, or a trifle over 50 per cent. During those years, too, the organization had given training and opportunity to Roland Young, Katherine Cornell, Rollo Peters, Jose Ruben, Frank Conroy, Margaret Mower, Glen Hunter, Marjory Vonnegut, and other actors later to figure on our stage. It had provided a chance at literary expression to Philip Moeller, Zoe Akins, Lewis Beach, and to some extent Eugene O'Neill and Susan Glaspell, though they belong rather to the Provincetown Players. It brought Lee Simonson into the fold as a scene designer, and also gave practice to Rollo Peters and Robert Edmond Jones. It trained Edward Goodman and Philip Moeller as directors. It accustomed a public, small perhaps, to look with interest on experimental work, and to relish the unusual, work done for the sheer joy of the doing. Finally, it left among the workers themselves a sense of incompletion, of a vision striven for but not attained, a realization of mistakes, but a belief nonetheless that the vision was a sound one, that in a spirit of coöperation and united purpose some day it was not unattainable.

III

Founding the Guild

ONLY a month after the Armistice, while several workers in the Washington Square Players were still in the army, Lawrence Langner suggested to Philip Moeller and Helen Westley that an effort should be made to get the group together in order to start a new art theatre. Meeting with a favorable response, Langner wrote several letters to a number of his former colleagues of the Washington Square Players, as well as some others who had been interested in the art theatre movement, and called a meeting at the home of Josephine A. Meyer, who had been a member of the Players, to discuss resuming in some form the attempt to establish in New York the kind of theatre these young people believed in. At this meeting, held on December 19, 1918, there were present Josephine Meyer, Helen Westley, Edna Kenton, Philip Moeller, Rollo Peters, and Lawrence Langner. Plans were discussed, and a basic policy laid down, included in which there was strongly and successfully urged by Rollo Peters and others, as a new basis of operations, a strict professionalism in the acting company.

Another and larger meeting was held which Helen Freeman, Lee Simonson and Justus Sheffield also attended. It was then proposed, but voted down, to try to raise a fund of $40,000 before beginning operations. But some money there had to be, even the most reckless admitted, so Mr. Langner contributed $500 and Maurice Wertheim, on his return from Europe, contributed a like sum. Mr. Justus Sheffield also made a contribution.

At a later meeting, the name "The Theatre Guild" was chosen, obviously suggested by the mediaeval trade guilds with coöperative organization and pride in craftsmanship.

Before any definite plans could be made for an opening, however, a theatre had to be secured, not an easy task in an era of high rentals. Daly's Theatre, by that time left behind, a mournful relic, by the northward march of Broadway, was vacant, and both because of its physical construction and its traditions appealed greatly to the new Guild. Reluctantly, however, they abandoned the idea of renting it and beginning their new venture in the home of the last of the great stock companies. The cost of upkeep was too great. But there was another theatre left behind by the northward trek, smaller than Daly's, that offered a possible solution. This was the Garrick, on West 35th Street, built originally by Harrigan and Hart, at one time leased by Richard Mansfield, and remembered by New York playgoers as the house where they saw Gillette in "Secret Service," Crane as *David Harum*, and that single famous performance by Arnold Daly of "Mrs. Warren's

Profession" which so shocked the New York police. During the Great War the house had been leased by Otto H. Kahn as a home for Jacques Copeau, looked upon by many as a savior of dramatic art in tradition-ridden France. But as France was too busy saving her life to bother about dramatic art, Mr. Kahn helped Copeau tide over the lean times by bringing him to America. For his season at the Garrick the house had been much altered. The stage boxes had been removed and something approximating the old-time forestage doors substituted. The upper balcony had been closed off, and the stage itself stripped to the bare bones, for it was a part of salvation *à la* Copeau that the audience must see the brick walls of the theatre.

With the ending of the War, Copeau returned to France, and the theatre was tenantless. Mr. Kahn, who has aided many artistic experiments, and took a friendly interest in the Washington Square Players, was now appealed to. He consented to sublet the Garrick to the Guild for two Spring productions, at a figure far below that asked for any Broadway house, and he further offered to take part payment in stock for weeks when the profits might not be sufficient to meet the full charge. Mr. Kahn's possession of the Garrick at this time, and his friendliness, were of immense advantage to the Guild. It is difficult to see how they could have made a successful start had the problem of a small theatre, conveniently situated, and at a low rental, not thus been met. He was as near to a patron as they ever had.

The Spring of 1919 was now on the way. A theatre was

secured. The Guild was formally organized, consisting of the following "Board of Managers," Rollo Peters, designated as director, Philip Moeller, Helen Freeman, Helen Westley, Justus Sheffield, Lawrence Langner and Lee Simonson. Theresa Helburn was Play Representative for the organization, but not yet a member of the Board. Maurice Wertheim had not yet returned to America from a war mission to Persia, or doubtless he would have been included. He was made a member of the Board a month after the opening of the Guild's first production. All that remained was to pick a play, get a cast, secure a list of subscribers, and make a production — all on a promised $1,000. Surely no smaller acorn ever sprouted an oak.

The choice of the first play was a matter of much debate, especially as the Guild was determined to function as a guild, taking no step that was not agreed upon by all, and designating powers to individual members always under the control of the Board as a whole. It was the general opinion that a long play should be offered, not a bill of one-act dramas, but otherwise the Guild as yet could not be said to have had a policy to guide their choice, other, of course, than the policy of picking a good play, and preferably one ignored by the commercial theatre. They finally chose Benavente's "Bonds of Interest." Philip Moeller was designated to direct it, and Rollo Peters, with his powers as director of the organization perhaps somewhat too vaguely defined to please one convinced of the "czar" theory of production, made the settings and costumes. Meanwhile the campaign for subscribers to the proposed Spring season of two plays was going on — without overworking the clerical staff. Less than $1,000 was taken in, which, of course, had to be listed as a liability.

Under the circumstances, Peters achieved wonders. Working largely with the odds and ends of scenery left behind by Copeau, he made sets with atmospheric charm, and working with the humblest and cheapest material, he devised costumes of beauty. For Miss Amelia Somerville he made a truly gorgeous cloth-of-gold gown, which hung in rich, heavy folds — out of oilcloth and gilt radiator paint. It was, to be sure, almost unbearably hot and heavy for the actress, but from the front served magnificently — until she sat down, at the opening performance. Then, when she tried to rise, she discovered to her horror that the chair was coming, too. But she eased herself out at last, and made her exit from the stage — disclosing to the audience large patches of oilcloth where the gold had been. A quaint incident, which might have happened to George Kelly's "Torchbearers."

Monday, April 14, 1919, was the date when the Guild began to function, and this was the first cast which ever played under their direction, in "Bonds of Interest."

Leander	Rollo Peters
Crispin	Augustin Duncan
Innkeeper	C. Hooper Trask
First Servant	Michael Carr
Second Servant	John Wilson

Harlequin	Walter Geer
Captain	Charles Macdonald
Maria	Beatrice Wood
Dona Sirena	Helen Westley
Columbine	Edna St. Vincent Millay
Laura	Kate Morgan
Risela	Mary Blair
Polichinelle	Dudley Digges
Wife of Polichinelle	Amelia Somerville
Silvia	Helen Freeman
Pantaloon	Leon Cunningham
Doctor	Henry Herbert
Secretary	Paul Lane
Constable	Jose Madrones

The members of that cast played for $25 a week, and a promise of sharing in the mythical profits, which means that most of the professionals in it were actuated by the same idealism as the Guild. Miss Westley, of course, was a member of the Guild. Dudley Digges, familiar with the problems of the Abbey Theatre, was interested in the experiment and valuable to it, and he has, with few and brief breaks, remained an invaluable member of the Guild company ever since. Miss Edna St. Vincent Millay, however, probably had no intention of becoming a professional actress. Her presence in that first cast is rather an indication of the creative background from which the Guild emerged.

But in spite of the attractive settings and the kindly welcome of the critics, "Bonds of Interest" languished. Possibly it is not so good a play as the Guild had thought. Possibly their company was not equal to the task of bringing it to a warm enough life to attract the public. Certainly the Guild was not yet an established institution, with public confidence behind it. And the production languished. It hung on for four weeks, the actors' salaries being first paid out of the original contributed capital, which soon gave out. After that Mr. Langner advanced additional funds, which kept the theatre going until Maurice Wertheim returned from abroad, shared the burden of the expense with him, and offered such additional help as might be needed.

The Guild, of course, had obligated itself to give two plays that Spring, and they proposed to do it, though it must have seemed to them at the time like nailing their flag to the mast and going down with colors flying. For the second offering they chose " John Ferguson," an unknown play of middle class, tragic realism, by an author quite unknown to America, St. John Ervine. It was a good play, and one certainly neglected by the commercial theatre, but it most certainly did not look like a popular success, especially when produced late in the Spring, at a half forgotten, side street theatre. Even its choice had an element of accident. Mr. Langner came across it in Brentano's, and remembered the author from his London days, when they were both members of the West London Parliament. "At that time Ervine was an Irish Socialist," Langner says, "but being from Belfast he was against all the other Socialists. That was the memory I had of him as I opened the book."

The First Ten Years

The Guild all agreed on the play, and cabled to Ervine. He demanded an advance payment of $1,000, as it later turned out upon the advice of G. B. Shaw, who said, "Get your money first." The Guild didn't have the $1,000, but they had sufficient powers of persuasion to win Ervine over at last, and the play was rushed into rehearsal. Rollo Peters again designed the setting, building it from odds and ends in the theatre storeroom, and spending only $300. Augustin Duncan, a brother of Isadora Duncan, staged the play. When it opened, on May 12, 1919, it is a fact that the Theatre Guild had exactly $19.50 of working capital left, to operate their theatre on. The emotions with which they watched the public reception of that production on its opening night, and read the papers the next morning, can hardly be described. Failure meant the end of their dreams. It meant, as we can see now, the setting back of the theatrical clock in America. It was truly a momentous occasion in our playhouse.

Again let us print the cast, as a roll of honor:

John Ferguson	Augustin Duncan
Sarah Ferguson	Helen Westley
Andrew Ferguson	Rollo Peters
Hannah Ferguson	Helen Freeman
James Caesar	Dudley Digges
Henry Withrow	Gordon Burby
Clutie	Henry Herbert
Sam Mawthinney	Walter Geer
Sargeant	Michael Carr

The Theatre Guild

"John Ferguson" did not fail. It was an immediate, and a deserved success. It was, of course, the type of play which an American company could understand and do justice to, without preliminary training together, and it was illusively staged by Mr. Duncan and imparted rich and genuine emotion. Its success was further enhanced, too, by the famous Actors' strike, which took place that Summer. Equity succeeded in closing every legitimate theatre in New York, except the Garrick. But the Guild they did not offer to molest. Quite the contrary. Equity highly approved of the coöperative organization of the Guild company. So for many weeks the only play which anybody in New York could witness was "John Ferguson," and business profited thereby. The actors actually received their small percentages, Mr. Kahn got his rent, and the Guild began to lay aside a few dollars as a production fund for the next season.

But the Garrick Theatre, with the second balcony closed off, seated less than 600 people, and hence it was impossible to make much money in it. With their second production, therefore, the Guild were confronted with a problem. They had a success on their hands. They had what Broadway calls a "property" capable of yielding them a much larger return than they were getting. Having made their first production on a shoe string and their second on less than that, and having gone through the agony of facing extinction if it failed, for lack of capital to tide them over, they knew only too well the need of a working fund if they were to continue to produce good plays and pay their bills.

But, on the other hand, if they moved "John Ferguson" to a larger Broadway theatre for a run, while they would increase their income, they would also tie up their actors. They might have to recruit a whole new company for the next production, losing the gain the first company had made by playing together. They would seem to be going out into open competition with the very theatre they scorned: they would seem to lose something of their independence and idealism. While "John Ferguson" was running at the Garrick, the Guild managers held stormy meetings, debating this problem pro and con.

The councils of financial independence finally won, for the Guild came to feel that the artistic independence which comes from a resident and permanent company can only be had on the basis either of subsidy or reserve capital. Subsidy they did not want. Quite the contrary. They wanted to be self-supporting and obligated to nobody. Accordingly, after 66 performances at the Garrick, "John Ferguson" was moved intact to the Fulton Theatre, on July 7, to harvest the returns of a larger auditorium. Certain of their well wishers cried out "Commercialism!" in shocked accents. And commercialism, in a sense, it certainly was. But commercialism sometimes means paying your bills. The Guild wanted some assurance it could pay its bills during the next season. It was not afraid of poverty, but it wanted permanence for its experiment, it didn't want to go under with the first heavy failure. It is quite possible that if the Guild had been organized under the prevalent theory of a czar director, and that director had been, as most likely he would have been, a zealous idealist, such a compromise would have been rejected. It was the result of long debate among all the managers, and represented finally the group sentiment. It is an excellent illustration of the pragmatic advantages of the group organization, in which practical counsel can have its full weight.

As a matter of record, "John Ferguson" ran at the Fulton for but 65 more performances, to August 30, so the company was not necessarily broken up, even though disassociated from the Garrick for a time.

IV

Six Characters in Search of an American Author

WHEN the preliminary announcements went out for the season of 1919–20, the first full season of the Guild, the name Augustin Duncan was substituted for that of Justus Sheffield on the Board of Managers, which otherwise remained the same. Rollo Peters was still denominated the " director." The changes were significant, and other changes followed until the Board assumed its present personnel. While they were of very minor interest to the public, no doubt, they were of the utmost importance to the success of the experiment, because that experiment was based on the group idea of production, with each member of the group finally functioning not as an individual, but as an agent of the entire Board. Individual taste and opinion was desirable, and was usually rampant, in the group deliberations, but when once an agreement had been reached, either in the choice of a play or the formation of a policy or even some minor detail, it was the duty of the individual cheerfully to do his assigned part for the good of the whole. To function under such conditions requires, of course, a peculiar temperament, and an unusual degree of friendly feeling and mutual thinking in the group. Each individual, above all, must be in full sympathy with the idea of group production and believe heartily that it is possible to run an art theatre under that system, if not indeed that it is the best system. So one of the two major concerns of the Guild in its early days was to find and weld together just the right people for its internal organization.

Its other great problem in its early days was to find American plays. When the Board assumed its final form, they became indeed six characters in search of an American author, and what they accomplished for American playwrighting may well prove, in time, to be a landmark of their early accomplishment.

That statement, I am well aware, will be challenged in various quarters. It will be said that there was little in the Guild's early repertoire to suggest that they had any interest at all in American authors. It will be said that they did not " take a chance " on O'Neill till other producers had made him famous, that they did not experiment with untried American dramas nor even produce the work of established native dramatists. Their tastes and their theatrical interest led them to European work. Nor can such comment be refuted by listing the Guild's early productions. It is perfectly true that the taste of the Guild directors was European in so far as it was for plays which combined theatrical effectiveness with some definite distinction of manner and still more some definite intellectual point. To produce American plays merely because they were American did not interest them at all, then or later. But being Americans themselves, and recognizing the greater intrinsic interest and value in native workmanship, for one's own countrymen, they naturally hoped constantly for native plays which could meet their test of fitness. Even had the acknowledged successful American dramatists of 1919 been writing such plays — which they were not — the Guild could hardly have produced them in the first season or two, for the simple reason that they were an experimental group, with a small theatre, and dedicated to make five or six productions a year. Therefore the dramatist would have hesitated to give his work to them, when the commercial playhouse could offer him the chance of larger royalties and a longer run. At the same time, they could not experiment with undeveloped native work, however promising, as an amateur group could do, because they were definitely pledged to the subscribers to produce finished entertainment. If they didn't do so, they would lose the subscribers and their theatre would go on the rocks. It was not, in their minds, at any time, an experimental theatre in the sense of trying out new, undeveloped work. It was an experiment in establishing a theatre dedicated to good drama on a permanent basis, and part of their pride in being self-supporting was, and is, based on the belief that by depending upon the public for support you keep yourself anchored to the consolidated artistic gains of the present, however much you may reach out toward the future.

Accordingly the Guild had to endure more or less in silence the frequent charges that they were "un-American" and to go ahead proving that good drama, written with distinction and intellectual point, would pay in America, and especially would pay in their theatre, hoping that ultimately American authors of capacity would write such drama, and be willing to submit it to them. If you like, their influence was indirect. But it was an influence, and a profound one. Ultimately American authors of capacity did write such plays, and submitted them to the Guild, gladly, hopefully, and submitted them to other managers as well, who produced them, too, because the Guild had proved that it would pay. The Guild was a profound influence in bringing the American drama out of the slump that had followed the first hopeful decade of this century.

Some reader may ask at this point why the members of the Guild did not write such plays themselves, since three of them, at least, had proved their capacity as dramatists. They did not because they early realized the danger to their organization of personal exploitation of any kind. It was safer and saner, in a theatre conducted by a group for an abstract ideal, not to inject so personal an element as the production of a member's play. That Philip Moeller, for example, who had shown much promise as a dramatist, should almost entirely abandon his writing to produce other men's plays for the good of the Guild, is an excellent measure of the devotion which has gone into this theatre from all its directors.

The first play of the first full season was Masefield's Japanese tragedy, "The Faithful," produced by Augustin Duncan with beautiful and ingenious settings by Lee Simonson, employing screens to excellent advantage. It was made on October 13, 1919, and there were 500 subscribers, a gain of 350 over the first Spring season. These subscribers hardly filled the theatre for one night, but the play ran for 48 performances, not at all a bad record for a modern poetic play. And during its run certain changes were made in the Board of Managers. Rollo Peters and Augustin Duncan both dropped out of the organization.

Their loss, of course, was regrettable, as each had already contributed much to the nascent theatre, but it was no less inevitable. Both men cherished perfectly legitimate and honorable personal ambitions, the one as an actor, the other as a director. The Guild, as an abstract ideal of a theatre, was not so close to either as it was to the other managers. Mr. Duncan especially, moreover, was theoretically opposed to the group idea of production, inclining strongly to the czar theory — one supreme director, not a coöperative policy. As each was called upon, under the Guild system, to subordinate his personal conviction to the group ideal, the break became inevitable. It was in no sense a quarrel. The organization was merely shaking down to a membership completely harmonious in theory and aim. Without that complete harmony of theory and aim, it could not function.

On November 25 the second play of the season was produced, this time by Philip Moeller. It was an American play, too, a dramatization of "The Rise of Silas Lapham," and in an attempt to attract patronage the Guild engaged James K. Hackett to play the leading part. This was a mistake, both of policy and casting. Hackett, a strutting, romantic actor of the gay 'nineties, and latterly, after inheriting a fortune, an experimenter in Shakespeare, was no longer a "draw" at the box office, nor had he ever been a good choice for Howells' realistic story. He was, however, a star, with a dominant personality, and concentrated emphasis which should have been distributed. The Guild learned a rather costly lesson. It was the last time a star actor ever appeared in one of their productions. The play was kept on for 48 performances, until, on January 5, 1920, the third play of the season was shown, Tolstoi's "Power of Darkness," produced by that fine old German artist, Emanuel Reicher, in settings by Simonson. Reicher, of course, was thoroughly equipped by training to produce this type of Continental realism, and by engaging him the Guild rightly felt they could learn much. They were, too, admirers of Tolstoi and considered his plays the sort of drama it was their special job to give hearing to. And who shall say that by giving hearing to such a tragedy of ignorance as "Power of Darkness" they did not hasten the day when

The First Ten Years

Paul Green could, in " The Field God," attempt an American tragedy of ignorance?

But the production was very nearly a tragedy of ambition for the Guild. It did not attract the public in profitable numbers, and when the managers met with Mr. Reicher in the " library " of the Garrick (which was a small room in the basement) to discuss the all important question of what they should produce next, in an effort to keep going, they had exactly $100 in the bank, and bills of $200 to meet. With this balance sheet before them the question of the next play was somewhat more than academic, nor did the meeting open with happy hilarity. Mr. Reicher, prowling along the book shelves amid the encircling gloom, suddenly took down a volume and, passing it to the directors, said, " Why don't you produce this? " The play was " Jane Clegg," by St. John Ervine. It was less than a year since Ervine's " John Ferguson " had enabled them to weather the first season, and naturally they were predisposed to his work. The play was at once read, agreed upon, and speedily put into rehearsal. The cast was small, the setting (by Simonson) simple, the realism of the play intelligible to American audiences, the story moving. It looked like a good choice.

It was. Staged by Mr. Reicher, with Dudley Digges, back with the Guild, as *Henry Clegg*, Margaret Wycherly as *Jane*, and Henry Travers as the *Bookie*, the play was singularly illusive and moving, and, like most illusive and moving performances in the theatre, found a public. In fact, it ran for 177 performances, till July 24, so that the final subscription performances, of Strindberg's "Dance of Death" (the two parts condensed into one), was given on two successive Sunday evenings, for the subscribers alone.

It was during the stressful period before the production of "Jane Clegg" that the Guild made its final change in personnel, and found at last the exact combination which could function together. Miss Helen Freeman withdrew from the Board, and Miss Theresa Helburn, who as Play Representative had for some time been an unofficial guest at Board meetings, was elected to fill Rollo Peter's position as executive and made a member of the Board. This meant that Miss Westley was the only professional player left on the Board, which had contained four, and it meant one more director with an academic and amateur background. Also, it is only fair to point out, it meant one more director who was not dependent on the theatre for a livelihood, and could afford to struggle with the Guild at the infinitesimal salaries the Board of Managers were then taking for themselves.

The second full season opened with a small but encouraging increase in the number of subscribers — an increase of 800, making the total 1,300. That was still far from enough to insure a production against heavy loss if it failed to attract the public, but it did ensure an interested audience for the first three or four performances, which is of great advantage to any play. No American drama had yet appeared, and the season opened with David Pinski's

The First Ten Years

Yiddish comedy, "The Treasure," translated by Ludwig Lewisohn, staged by Emanuel Reicher, in sets by Simonson. Among Pinski's claims to fame is the fact that after studying three years at Columbia for a Ph.D. he forgot to go to his meeting with the examiners because he became absorbed in finishing a play. "The Treasure," written in 1906, produced by Reinhardt in Berlin in 1910, and well known to drama students, is concerned with the Jewish proletariat in Europe, and makes rather bitter fun of money worship. It is an interesting work, but possibly remote from American audiences, and difficult to translate. The Guild could extract but 34 performances from it, and then Ervine again came to their rescue.

Not this time with a play of his own, however. The previous June he had suggested to G. B. Shaw that this odd American theatre, which had done so well with two of his neglected dramas, might produce Shaw's new play, "Heartbreak House," which because of the wartime passions Shaw's opinions had aroused could find no producer on either side of the water. Shaw's reply was that he doubted if there existed in New York a management " bold enough and clever enough to know that the alternative to pleasing an audience for two hours is to put the utmost strain upon their attention for three, and send them home exhausted but impressed." The Guild were certainly clever enough (the amateur proving a much better showman than the showman) to know that it would be a great feather in their cap to make a first production of a Shaw play, whether it amused or exhausted. They closed the deal, and announced the premier for their October opening. The reason they opened with "The Treasure" instead was that G. B. S. forbade them to proceed till the Presidential election was over. The Guild protested that to wait meant to lose all the "superlative" actors they had engaged.

"Inexorable; Shaw," came back a cable. A letter followed. "Better to produce 'Heartbreak House' with the first cast you could pick out of the gutter on Nov. 15, than to produce it on Oct. 15 with Sarah Bernhardt, the two Guitrys, Edwin Booth, John Drew, Maude Adams, Mary Pickford and Charlie Chaplin."

So it was not produced until after election! Dudley Digges was the director, and Lee Simonson made the settings, which as I noted did not depart in any essential from Shaw's minute descriptions. "And should not," was Simonson's rejoinder. "Shaw's directions are 100 per cent." The truth of that I was later somewhat painfully to realize when I saw a Shaw comedy acted in a constructivist set. A shrewd and sensible respect for an author's style and mood has always been a distinguishing mark of Mr. Simonson's stage designs, and he has never obtruded himself or his theories in front of a competent dramatist.

The magic of Shaw as a drawing card, and the intrinsic interest of the play, kept this production running for 129 performances, to February 26, 1921. During its run, which marked the beginning of the happy relations between Shaw and the Guild and also gave to the Guild something of international prestige, an American play was put on for six matinees, "John Hawthorne," by David Liebovitz. It was a play about the Southern Highlanders, who have since been much exploited, but it did not prove that the native dramatists were yet ready to give the Guild the plays it desired.

On February 28, 1921, A. A. Milne's "Mr. Pim Passes By" was produced, with Laura Hope Crews as *Olivia* and Erskine Sanford in the title role. The discovery of this play was made by Maurice Wertheim, and the happy choice of Miss Crews was made by Miss Helburn, who has since made many happy choices in the selection of actors. The only play of Milne's till then acted in America was "Belinda," which Miss Barrymore had tried. His work was practically unknown and was going begging from theatrical office to office. Since the success of "Mr. Pim," of course, he has not lacked for producers. The play was directed by Philip Moeller, who shared with Miss Crews a keen relish for its peculiar humor, and made a silken production — rippled silk.

The play, indeed, was so successful that again the Guild were faced with the problem whether to cut the run short to make way for their final production or move the company to another theatre and reap the profit. They compromised somewhat by changing certain members of the cast, so they could retain Miss Westley and Mr. Digges especially at the Garrick, and sent the play up to the Henry Miller Theatre. It ran for a total of 232 performances in New York, and then was turned over to a commercial manager,

The Theatre Guild

on a royalty basis, for a road tour. Meanwhile, at the Garrick, on April 20, the Guild produced a drama which was unusual in content, which called for a long cast, which required much ingenuity and imaginative quality in the staging, and which for several years had gone begging in New York. That play was Molnar's now famous "Liliom."

Simonson's sets, ingeniously simple but especially in the noted railroad embankment scene realizing with great felicity a three dimensional quality as well as pictorial charm and the right dramatic mood, were not only immediately appreciated but had a considerable and helpful influence over the Little Theatre workers throughout the country. Frank Reicher, a son of Emanuel, who directed the production, handled his crowded canvas well, filling it with lifelike animation, caught the humor, the fantasy, and the pathos, aided by excellent acting. The play was a huge success, and was transferred to the Fulton Theatre in May, where it ran till the following January, a total of 311 performances. It was then turned over to a road manager. The success of this play was not only helpful financially to the Guild; it also demonstrated with great vividness the popular appeal of an imaginative play, well mounted and acted, and heartened all writers and producers interested in creating such work. The play went into the repertoire of the Little Theatres, too, following its Guild success, and gave more than one amateur group a new standing in its community.

The First Ten Years

In May the Guild made a tentative gesture toward their far off goal of repertoire by staging a revival of "John Ferguson" at the Garrick, but the original cast was dispersed and the spirit could not be recaptured. It showed them, however, if they needed to be shown, the necessity of a permanent company before their dreams could be realized. The season ended with two performances for subscribers of Verhaeren's "The Cloister."

Out of the five public productions made that season, the Guild had scored three rousing popular successes, and those successes were plays of distinction. Three out of five is considered on Broadway an extraordinarily high average, but to have the three turn out to be plays which Broadway had scorned as unlikely to succeed was rather rubbing it in. Broadway began to pay more attention to what the Guild was doing. So did the public, for subscriptions to the next season nearly doubled in number.

And the next season began with an American play, by a young American author, which was experimental in form, pointed in purpose, and competent in execution — "Ambush" by Arthur Richman.

"Ambush" was staged by Robert Milton, opening on October 10, 1921. The scene of the play was Jersey City, the theme was the pressure of modern life and luxury on the lives of the humble, and the technical innovation consisted in telling the story entirely from the point of view of one character. It was not a masterpiece, but it was an intelligent attempt by a young American dramatist to produce the kind of work the Guild had been fighting for, and the Board were delighted when it ran at the Garrick till late in November and was still so popular that it could be moved to the Belmont, and finally complete 98 performances. Their crusade was bearing fruit.

V

Wrestling with "Methuselah"

MARKING time with a double bill from the French, "Boubouroche," a farce, and "The Wife with a Smile," both associated with the experimental playhouse of Paris, the Guild made ready for their boldest ventures to date, the first production anywhere of Shaw's Gargantuan drama, "Back to Methuselah," which had been published the previous Summer, and the first professional production in America of Andreiev's "He Who Gets Slapped," which had been produced with college amateurs by Alexander Dean at the University of Montana.

The Russian play came first, being exhibited on the tiny Garrick stage January 9, 1922, its many-peopled scene effectively handled by Simonson through the use of two stage levels, connected by stairs, so there was no sense of overcrowding. Those who probably know much better than I do exactly what Andreiev's play is about affirmed that the setting was, however, too rich and glamorous, and Robert Milton's direction too romantic. Andreiev, they said, was writing realistic fantasy, whatever that is, and meant his tawdry circus as an ironic snarl at the cosmos he despised. The people were frankly bewildered, but oddly enough they seemed to enjoy being bewildered by this play. They flocked to it in great numbers, and what the Guild had fully expected to be an interesting offering in the newer drama to their subscribers, and a valuable experience in meeting production problems for themselves, turned out to be a public success. In February it was moved to the Fulton Theatre, brought back to the Garrick in May, and chalked up 274 New York performances. It was perhaps the most striking illustration the Guild had yet made of the audience which exists for drama of unusual quality.

"Back to Methuselah," which followed hard on the Russian drama, was not a popular success, and probably never can be one, outside of China, where they don't mind their plays three days long. Yet its production marked a mile stone in the progress of the Guild, not alone for the prestige which it brought them, but for the practice it gave them in surmounting production difficulties and the lessons they learned about acting, soon to be reinforced by other lessons, till their purpose was inevitably expanded to include the achievement of a larger theatre and a permanent company picked not as types but as vivid yet versatile artists.

When the Guild, even in advance of publication, had asked Shaw for a contract to produce his "Gospel of Creative Evolution," he had replied, "A contract is unnecessary. It isn't likely that any other lunatics will want to produce it." When the book appeared, many readers agreed with him. Before the play reached the stage, some of the Guild managers and not a few of the cast were almost ready to agree, also.

To do the play at all required a long cast and numerous sets. But to do it within a limited budget, so that the losses would not be too great, required that the same actors appear in the various parts of the play, and that the sets be somehow simplified over the conventional scenery. If an actor were engaged for *Adam*, for example, and then not used again, he would have to be paid for his two weeks of idleness, till the first acts came around once more in the cycle, and other actors would have to be engaged for later roles — and paid. It was necessary to find players who could fit roles in all acts of the play, and who were, further, willing to undertake the labor of learning these roles — the equivalent of " getting up " three parts for a single engagement. As the minimum Guild salary was at that time much lower than on Broadway, and as the prospect of profits to share in were in this case practically non-existent, it can be seen that to cast the Shaw opus was no simple task, and that those actors who did finally appear in it were actuated by other motives than gain. The weeks of preparation (the Garrick remained dark for a fortnight before the opening, to get the stage ready) were tremendously busy ones, but there had hardly been a time in the history of the organization when everybody, including the actors, worked at such high pitch and yet so enthusiastically and harmoniously. To do the thing at all was a thrilling challenge, and in that spirit it was rehearsed.

The previous May, after the Guild had read the manuscript, Shaw had written:

"The second play will not mean Asquith and Lloyd George to your public; and so far it will not produce the effect it will produce here on the few people who have any sense of political personalities. But in "Fanny's First Play" the American public knew nothing about Walkley, Gilbert Cannan and A. E. Vaughan (for that matter very few people, outside a little ring in London, were any better informed). Nevertheless Trotter, Gunn and Vaughan went down just as well in America as here. I therefore believe that if Joyce Burge and Lubin fail here, they will fail everywhere; and if they succeed here they will succeed just as well in America. However that may be, the thing must stay as it is now. The job itself did itself that way and I cannot pull it to pieces and do it some other way.

"As to the first play, it produced such an astonishing effect when I read it to an audience consisting mostly of women that I never ventured on the experiment again. I gather that it missed fire with you. It may do so with your public; but I assure you it *can* explode with shattering consequences. To play it and the second play at the same performance is impossible. You will have to make up your mind to the three evenings and the two matinees. You must sell the tickets in batches of five, all five tickets on one sheet with perforated card divisions. If people buy them that way they will not throw them away. They may be bothered and disappointed by the first two plays as you expect; but their bewilderment will not take the form of throwing their tickets into the fire, especially if you charge enough for them. You can warn them that the dialogue in the Garden of Eden will last only an hour (or perhaps 50 minutes: you can time it at rehearsal) and that no assumptions must be made as to the duration of each part of the play. Mark: each part of the play, not each play. The wording of your programmes and announcements must always rub in the fact that what the public is going to see is one play, with sections of various lengths.

"Later on we can see about giving separate performances of the sections; but for the first ten performances (say) it must be impossible to take less than the whole dose."

Shaw's expectations as to the reception of Lubin and Joyce Burge were fulfilled, but the Guild for once did not yield to his scheme of three evenings and two matinees, partly because many of their subscribers could not come in the afternoon. They divided the drama into three sections, and played each section a week, in cycle. Parts I and II were played the first week, ending with the "Gospel of the Brothers Barnabas." The second week Parts III and IV were acted — an interminable evening they made! Finally, Part V finished the cycle. Then the whole play started again. To direct the first part, the Guild called in Miss Alice Lewisohn and Miss Agnes Morgan, from the Neighborhood Playhouse. To direct the second, they once more employed Frank Reicher. The final part was directed by Philip Moeller. Lee Simonson designed all the settings, which had not only to be built within a reasonable cost, but to be so devised that they could all be stored on the restricted Garrick stage. In a sense, this one play, then, presented many of the problems of repertoire.

To solve some of his problems, Mr. Simonson employed a German device, the Linnebach projector. This is a lamp without a lens, which can be placed against the back wall of the theatre and throw a picture painted on a glass slide upon a translucent drop only a few feet away, enlarging it to the full size of the drop. Thus the audience out front see a painted back drop which has an odd, luminous quality, and thus the theatre, with only one drop cloth to hang, and a set of painted slides, can go on changing scenes indefinitely if too much is not called for in front of the drop. For the Eden scene, Simonson threw on the drop a great, luminous tree, and in front placed merely a green mound. The projector was used again to back the second act of Part I, to furnish the land-and-seascape behind Burrin Pier, and to create shadow effects in the Temple scene. The Eden Tree, particularly, was an imaginative and striking design, towering luminous and misty over our First Parents as they sat on the mound below. But it may be that this very quality of luminosity in the light-projected backing was out of key; certainly it took something from the actors, and tended to silhouette them. At any rate, the projector has figured little in subsequent Guild productions, or elsewhere on our stage.

It will be noted that the curtain was announced for Parts

III and IV at 7:30, and the conclusion at 11:25. Not a little of that length was caused by the garrulity of the *Elderly Gentleman*, played by Albert Bruning in a make-up closely resembling G. B. S. himself. Mr. Bruning was an excellent actor, but rapidity of utterance was not a characteristic of his style; moreover, he was what is known as a "slow study." With the role of *Franklyn Barnabas* to learn in Part II, as well, he was hard put to master the endless outpourings of the *Elderly Gentleman*, and could not emit them with a rapidity which might possibly have mitigated the boredom of less worshipful members of the audience. Nor were his troubles lessened when Shaw finally consented to permit cuts in his text. It was harder still for poor Mr. Bruning to unlearn what he had just learned so painfully! But, in lesser degree, all the players found the task of committing their various roles, and having them ready for alternate presentation, a taxing business.

To the general public, Part II, which closed the first section of the play as the Guild divided it, was the most successful. A. P. Kaye and Claude King, thinly disguised as Lloyd George and Asquith (Mr. Kaye's make-up was almost ludicrously lifelike), were capital, in a scene full of typical Shavian comedy. Part II, "The Thing Happens," was also effective, with a decided thrill of suspense and excitement in the growing revelation of the *Bishop* and *Mrs. Lutestring*. But the endless scene on Burrin Pier unquestionably taxed the attention even of Guild theatregoers beyond the point of pleasure. Part V, played the third week, short as it was, and staged in a bright (almost operatic) set, could not quite pull them back. Indeed, the bold, imaginative quality of that scene, pictured by the reader, tames down perilously into fantastic makebelieve when reduced to the pasteboard and paint of the playhouse.

The Guild, of course, suffered still more in this method of production by the fact that a visitor to New York couldn't possibly see the whole play unless he was in town some part of three consecutive weeks, nor could anybody see it at all without paying much more than the price of one ordinary play, even at the reduced rates made for the complete cycle. Hearing rumors that it put a tremendous strain on an audience, people who might have ventured to try it for an evening hesitated to try it for three. As a result, it was acted but 25 times — 25 times for each of the three divisions, that is, making a total of 75 performances. Financially, because of its expensive cast and extensive sets, it was the Guild's heaviest loss up to this time. The loss, indeed, reached $20,000. Some time later Shaw wrote a letter to the manager who was hesitantly considering his translation of Trebitch's play to the effect that this manager did not sufficiently realize the value of Shaw's name. "The Theatre Guild," he said, "made $10,000 out of my name alone. They expected to lose $30,000 on their production of "Back to Methuselah," and only lost $20,000."

But in other ways it was the opposite of a loss. The prestige of producing, for the first time on any stage, this vast and supposedly unactable drama, by one of the world's foremost playwrights, and a drama, too, which he declared contained his religious Gospel to the world — the Gospel of Creative Evolution, was of enormous future benefit to the Guild. It gave added importance to their venture in the eyes both of America and Europe, and added assurance that they were ready to sacrifice profits in the interest of an important work of art. Further, it gave them valuable practice in trying to meet the problems of what amounted to handling three productions in rotation, in shifting actors from one part to another and back again, in simplification of scenery, and in creating, or attempting to create, unusual effects, or to realize situations — like those in Part V — far removed from the ordinary emotional reactions of men and women. The Guild will probably always look back upon this production as one of their milestones.

Certainly none of the actors who memorized the leading parts will ever forget it!

The last performance was on April 29. After this Shaw gave to the Guild the American option on all his plays and the right to release them for production.

On May 1, with some of the same actors in the cast who had just finished learning "Back to Methuselah," the Guild produced Arnold Bennett's "What the Public Wants." It wasn't.

But on May 21, starting with four special performances for subscribers, came a play which happily brought the season to a brilliant finish, and caught public attention, as well. It was Georg Kaiser's "From Morn to Midnight," translated by Ashley Dukes, and produced by Frank Reicher in seven scenes brilliantly designed in the impressionist style of the drama by Lee Simonson.

The first four special performances were followed by four regular performances at the Garrick, and then the production was moved to the larger Frazee Theatre, where it ran for 48 performances, till August 5. Coming as it did at the end of a New York season which had seen Eugene O'Neill's "Hairy Ape," this example of expressionism from the original German spring was a doubly interesting novelty. Simonson's odd and imaginative sets, too, were of much interest, the more because they were often achieved by very simple means, picking a part of the stage out of darkness, and letting the surrounding gloom (representing money saved on stage carpentering!) suggest the dark womb of scenes to come. The Linnebach projector was used to project a tree which writhed into a skeleton. The box at the velodrome was a high platform, under a searchlight, those on it looking into the rays as if into a lighted arena. But what was, perhaps, most stirring in the production was the driving pace at which Frank Reicher sent it along, like scenes shaping, dissolving, in a tortured mind. The play was curiously exciting, as well as novel, and was a fitting end to the Guild's most daring and experimental season.

VI

"Peer Gynt" and the Growing Need for a Permanent Company

WHEN the fifth season opened, in October 1922, the Guild had 6,000 subscribers, as a result of the vivid and interesting productions they had made. Six thousand people paying their money in advance for a whole season of plays was something new in our theatre, and something not to be scorned. It represented roughly an advance sale of $60,000, and was unmistakable proof that a large public wanted the kind of plays which interested the Guild. The season before, O'Neill's "Hairy Ape," as we mentioned, had been produced on Broadway, though the Guild and O'Neill were yet to adjust certain perhaps temperamental differences which kept his work off their stage. Producers like Arthur Hopkins were finding their way easier. The Guild had already produced "Ambush," and had now on the hooks another and more experimental native play, soon to be exhibited. Our authors were beginning to attempt the kind of plays the Guild was interested in, and beginning to submit them to the Guild. Moreover, other managers in the commercial theatre were taking heart and producing such plays. A chapter in Guild history was closing. Certainly they no longer had to ask, " Is this the kind of play the commercial theatre will not do? " as one of their tests of fitness, nor had they any longer to demonstrate that strict adherence to high standards of production and of literary merit is appreciated by the public and is good business. The public was increasingly supporting them by assured subscriptions. That task was done. They would have either to stand still, or to move on toward new ends. And what those ends were experience very soon demonstrated.

The season opened on October 9 with Karel Capek's satirical drama of the machine age, " R. U. R.," a production notable for Mr. Moeller's skilled direction and Mr. Simonson's hauntingly suggestive costume and make-up for the Robots. Six years later this play was restored to the repertoire in a new production by Rouben Mamoulian. It had a run of 182 performances, at the Garrick and Frazee Theatres, when first shown. "R. U. R." was followed by Milne's " The Lucky One," not a very good play, and certainly not adapted to exhibiting the best powers of a new director the Guild had just imported from Europe, from whom they hoped to learn. That director was Theodore Komisarshevsky, brother of the famous Russian actress, Vera Komisarshevsky. After her death, just before the war, he had conducted a theatre named in her honor, in Moscow, after his own ideas of " expressionism and synthesis." In 1919 he went to London and made several productions for the Everyman Theatre and mounted six operas at Covent Garden. It was especially to aid them in their projected revival of "Peer Gynt" that the Guild now brought him to New York, oddly enough the same winter that the Moscow Art Theatre elected to come here.

The second production he made for the Guild was of Claudel's "The Tidings Brought to Mary," sensitively translated by Louise Morgan Sill. Here, of course, he had material much better adapted to his production methods, and working with Simonson as designer, he evolved almost a series of tableaux on low platforms under a specially constructed proscenium with a pointed arch, and before neutral backgrounds. The long, flowing costumes, the soft play of tinted lights, and the groupings under this pointed arch, gave something the effect of a stained-glass cathedral window come to life in three dimensions — an effect, of course, peculiarly in harmony with the drama. A public for this play in latter day New York, however, was strictly limited, and the Guild's December mail was not confined to Christmas greetings.

One subscriber wrote to the Guild, "Will the significance of its beautiful message be lost on the Babbitts and Calibans of this highly materialistic and sophisticated age? What a pity if it should!" But other subscribers were not so pleased. One man wrote, ". . . I know four people who were so disgusted that they said they would not renew their subscriptions. Of course, I know that the public has refused to see the play; but what I cannot understand is how you could ever have inflicted such a monstrosity on your friends, the subscribers. My only satisfaction is that I shall probably not live long enough to again see a play so nasty and so disgusting."

On February 5, 1923, came the long planned revival of "Peer Gynt," a play which had not been seen in New York since Mansfield's production almost twenty years before. Archer's translation was used, cut to fifteen scenes, the omissions being most numerous in the last act, where unfortunately the rapid succession of scenes is most essential to the play. Mr. Simonson designed the settings and costumes, Joseph Schildkraut, who had done so well as *Liliom*, was engaged for *Peer*, and all the theatre's limited resources were taxed to the utmost to rehearse and handle so large a production.

Wrestling with " Peer Gynt " is a severe test of any theatre and company. William Winter, whose opinion of Ibsen was hardly flattering, says in his life of Mansfield, " The whole prodigious burden of animating, sustaining and impelling the deadly dulness and gelid inertia of the piece was borne by him [Mansfield] " — and the " prodigious burden " undoubtedly hastened that great actor's end. But much water had flowed past the Battery since 1907. The Guild and its director approached the problem of the play from other angles than Mansfield, and in some ways with greater resources. They had, for example, command over more suggestive and flexible scenery and lights, enabling them to reduce the stage waits, and to bring the visual elements of the play more into the mood of bizarre fantasy and poetry. The director, too, worked to create with his crowds, his movement, his separate scenes, a constant texture at once of reality and out of it, that should have a style as individual as the play it was fitted to. But, when all is said, "Peer Gynt" is *Peer Gynt,* and on the actor of that role, as William Winter remarked, falls the "prodigious burden" of "animating, sustaining and impelling" what is doubtless a great poem, but can be an unequal and at times not very absorbing play. Mr. Schildkraut was not equal to the task. Chosen because of his excellent performance of *Liliom,* he was here faced with one of the great tests, a role which requires ample and sustained energy, romantic sweep, poetic suggestion, ironic humor, and deep intellectual understanding. When Mansfield drove his old mother up to St. Peter's gate, it was a superb revelation of *Peer's* self-centred but overmastering imagination, and also it was a piece of sheer folk poetry and a theatrical tour de force which carried the audience aloft through the very roof of the theatre, and then dropped them back limp in their chairs. In the Guild production the scene went for little. The contrast was still greater, however, in Act V, at once the most difficult and profoundest act of the play. The Guild production, unlike Mansfield's, omitted the shipwreck, which so vividly and picturesquely brings the aged sinner back to his native land, shows him unchanged, and begins that final bombardment of strange apparitions which mark *Peer's* process of finding himself out. All the act thereafter is thrilling (or should be), with the rising desperation of this tragi-comic hero as he peels himself, like the onion, to find a core which isn't there, and all the "symbolism" of this act is but the expression, as Shaw long ago pointed out, of things which cannot be said literally. To catch this throb of rising desperation, to make each meeting with *Lean One* or *Button Moulder* the drama of a stricken soul, to bring out the final catastrophe in that last great outbreak, and then the stumbling slump into blind *Solveig's* lap, is the task not only of the producer but even more of the chief actor. It must be acted greatly, or it is mere puzzlement and disjointed fantasy. The Guild's Hall of the Troll King was far better realized than Mansfield's. The Guild, too, restored the Mad House scene, and made it a thing of uncanny suggestion. But when they reached the last act they bungled, partially by attempting too great a compression of scenes (only two were used), but chiefly because they lacked a leading actor who could rise to the great occasion, or even sufficient secondary ones to catch the grim suggestion, and strike the overtones of meaning.

I do not mean that the Guild production was a failure. It had many high merits, and the public liked it so well that it ran for 121 performances, being moved later to a larger theatre. Probably this is the longest run on record for this play. But it is one thing to please the public, and another to satisfy yourself. If the Guild managers were inclining toward self-satisfaction, they were checked by Stanislavsky, director of the Moscow Art Theatre, then playing in

The First Ten Years

New York. From their earliest Washington Square days, the Moscow Art Theatre had been a beacon to them, and when Stanislavsky, tall, gray, grave and patrician, sat through their "Peer Gynt" and then told them that their production had only "surface," they listened humbly and thoughtfully. Surface is not enough to bring a masterpiece to life; there must be the soul of acting beneath the surface, and in a theatre hoping to keep masterpieces in its repertoire this must be achieved by a permanent company of well trained, intelligent and ambitious players. The Guild, of course, needed nobody to confirm their need for a more ample stage and auditorium, if they were to handle such a play as "Peer Gynt" and do anything else at all with the stage, at the same time, or if they were to accommodate enough spectators to pay the bills. In other words, their ambition was outrunning their organization. They needed a permanent acting company, and they needed a new theatre large enough to support it. Obviously, that was the next step, and how they took it is another chapter.

They did, however, have a nucleus of players who were looked upon by the public now as Guild actors, and it is noticeable that the productions in which these players took the leading parts were very often the most successful. That was true of the next production, Elmer Rice's American expressionistic drama, "The Adding Machine." What Mr. Moeller, the director, may have learned from Komisarshevsky no outsider can say, but he certainly pointed its native idiom as no alien could have done. Simonson's settings were ingenious and imaginative, especially the scenic dramatization of *Zero's* brain storm, the acting was vivid (the parts, of course, are lacking in overtones, which is a great deficiency of the play), and the whole production was heartening to those who desired to see our stage stride along with that of Europe.

The last play of the season was Shaw's "Devil's Disciple," which Mansfield had originally disclosed to the American public in 1897. It was odd that the Guild should have invited two comparisons with this actor in a single season, but perhaps goes to show that when you are working for a rich and rounded theatre you cannot escape the great traditions. They had, alas, no Mansfield for the role of *Dick Dudgeon*, but the record would be lamentably incomplete if it did not include a mention of Roland Young's performance of General Burgoyne, the only one I ever saw in which the actor contrived absolutely to realize Shaw's stage direction, "This retort almost reconciles Gen. Burgoyne to the loss of America." The production ran all summer, and inaugurated the Guild's custom of an annual Shaw revival.

VII

The Bond Sale for the New Guild Theatre

THE Guild, in its origins, was an amateur theatre. It was a part of that movement in America during the first quarter of the present century to find an outlet for dramatic self-expression, both in colleges and communities — a movement which may possibly prove to be the salvation of the spoken drama in many sections of the country. And the Guild's achievement of a theatre building of its own was made possible by community support. The Managers only too well realized their need of a proper theatre, with a larger seating capacity than the Garrick and a much ampler stage. Without it, indeed, they could not capitalize their successes without dispersing their players: they could not play repertoire; they could not build up a permanent company which the directors of the Moscow Art Theatre had told them was their greatest need. Such a theatre they could not rent, even if it existed, as the charge would be too high. But how could they build it, with their limited funds, and limited credit?

And then a suggestion came to them, neither from

The Theatre Guild

Broadway nor Wall Street, but from the Theatre du Vieux Colombier in New Orleans, an amateur organization. Needing a new playhouse, this organization sold $60,000 worth of bonds to the interested and friendly community. The Guild now had behind them an interested and friendly community. Why couldn't they do the same thing in New York? Why couldn't they take New York theatregoers into partnership, as it were? To sell stock would mean a loss of control, but to sell bonds would mean merely to take advantage of good will, while retaining full control. Could they do it? Would New York respond? Were their friends confident enough of the Guild's future to back that confidence with money?

The subject was earnestly debated, and rough estimates made of what the new theatre would cost. At first they estimated $300,000 was needed. But it soon went up to $500,000, and then still higher. They would certainly need $500,000 in cash, as a start. They had 10,000 subscribers. Would 5,000 of them buy $100 bonds, or 500 of them buy $1,000 bonds? It was a gamble. But one thing was certain. The Guild had to have a new theatre or stagnate artistically, and this seemed to be the only promising way to achieve it.

Accordingly, on March 4, 1923, at its fourth birthday dinner at the Waldorf, the Guild made a public announcement of its purpose, and immediately thereafter set the campaign in motion. An executive committee was formed, consisting of Professor George P. Baker, Mrs. August Belmont, Mr. William M. Chadbourne, Mr. Walter Prichard Eaton, Miss Helburn, Mr. Otto H. Kahn, Mr. Langner, Mr. Walter Lippmann, Mr. Charles Riegelman, Mr. Louis Untermeyer, Mr. Allen Wardwell and Mr. Wertheim. This committee held its first meeting in a vacant loft adjoining the Garrick Theatre, and sat on packing cases, as no furniture had yet been installed. The nature of the bond issue was determined, and details of the drive arranged. At Mr. Wertheim's suggestion, the bonds, in denominations of $1,000, $500, and $100, were made 6 per cent cumulative income bonds; that is, no interest was obligatory in any year when it was not earned, but accumulated as a charge. (Incidentally, the Guild has always made the annual payments.) The bonds were to be secured by the equity on the new theatre, and to make them more attractive the Guild was required to set aside each year half of any profits for redemption of these bonds at 115, and to accumulate and maintain, as further security, an interest reserve fund equal to two years' interest on bonds outstanding. Obviously every effort was made to safeguard the investor, and to make the bonds a sound security. Nevertheless, it was still a gamble whether the public would buy them.

To sell these bonds, for the erection of a theatre on land not yet purchased, the Guild asked for volunteers from among its subscribers and friends. And instantly they had the happiest surprise of their career. Men and women came forward in droves, eager to help, to play a personal and active part in this new kind of theatre. The vacant loft was vacant no more. It hummed with activity. Fifteen teams, each of twenty salesmen and women, were organized under captains, and on April 2 went forth to sell.

Plans for teas, luncheons and dinners had already been made. Meetings had been arranged for in clubs and theatres. Prizes were offered to those workers selling the largest number of bonds, but nobody was permitted to sell more than $10,000 worth to any one person. There was a black board in headquarters, where returns were posted every night, and good natured rivalry ran high. In short, it had all the familiar aspects of a community drive.

The four weeks' campaign ended with a rally, ironically enough held in the Shubert Theatre. Six charming actresses stood behind adding machines and footed up the totals. Some of them got more than $100,000 out of the way, to be sure, but there was an accountant behind the scenes, and before the rally was over the drive had gone over the top. Ultimately, in fact, $600,000 worth of bonds were sold. There were but six subscriptions of $10,000. Of the 2,500 subscribers, about 1,500 purchased $100 bonds, and most of the rest did not go over a $1,000 purchase. It was a distinctly democratic distribution, and to a large extent represented the loyal interest of the rank and file of Guild subscribers. And it was made possible by the energetic and entirely volunteer toil of the selling teams, who found in this work a way in which they could be of practical service in the creation of a better theatre.

Perhaps the names at least of the prize winners among

these volunteers should be listed here, though they were merely the most persuasive among three hundred: Mrs. E. K. Bauer, Mr. Bela Blau, Mr. Alfred C. Bossom, Mrs. Joseph Deane, Mr. A. C. Hone, Mrs. Ned Kaufman, Mr. Benjamin Kaye, Miss Dorothy Kenyon, Mr. Abraham Mandelstam, Miss Sylvia Marks, Mr. Paul Moss, Mr. Warren P. Munsell, Miss Ethel R. Peyser, Mr. M. Raymond, Mr. Charles Riegelman, Mrs. Alfred Salemme and Miss Essie Waxelbaum.

No site, even, for the new theatre had been chosen before the money was in hand, but as soon as the drive was over a real estate committee was formed, and many sites investigated. Finally one on West 52nd Street was chosen and purchased. This street was not at the time in the theatrical district, though the trend seemed that way, and land values were less than elsewhere. They have almost doubled since the erection of the Guild Theatre. During the next few months the architects were busy on plans, and the corner stone was laid by Governor Smith on December 2, 1924. The new house was opened on April 5, 1925, almost exactly two years after the start of the bond campaign. Its final cost was more than $1,000,000, making a first mortgage necessary. It was not a real estate speculation, however, nor even a business concern. It was a monument to the valiant and uncommercial spirit of the new playhouse in America, a monument to the community support of sound, disinterested dramatic art.

VIII

*Carrying on at the Garrick—"Saint Joan"—
Down to Bed Rock Again*

Meanwhile the Guild had to keep going at the Garrick, with their minds full of the new playhouse plans, and worried by the new necessity of meeting large interest payments. They opened the season of 1923–24 with Galsworthy's "Windows," but it was not a success, lasting only till their subscribers, who now numbered 12,000, had seen it. Neither was the next play, a translation of H. R. Lenormand's "Les Ratés" ("The Failures"). This play, in settings ingeniously simplified by Simonson, and directed by Stark Young, the dramatic critic, brought to us a set of post-war Europeans spinning sad psychological subtleties, and intensely preoccupied with the problem of evil. It was not till late in December that the Guild's standby, G. B. Shaw, came to the rescue. On December 28, 1923, his "Saint Joan" was presented at the Garrick, for the first time on any stage. Through a misunderstanding, it had been rehearsed from a manuscript lacking the author's final revision, and on the opening night ran till midnight. The next morning the critics all bewailed its length, and bewailed the epilogue as needless, some even declaring that Shaw was doddering. The Guild, thoroughly terrified by the prospect of another failure, cabled Shaw for permission to cut, because, they said, suburbanites had to leave to catch their trains.

The reply was characteristic: " The old, old story. Begin at eight, or run later trains. Await final revision of play."

The revision soon came, but before it arrived the play was a success. It ran at the Garrick and then the Empire for 214 performances, and later, with a changed cast, was turned over to a road manager for a tour.

It is Shaw's habit, on receiving pictures of a production, to criticise freely and at length, and many of those criticisms are of value to future producers. For that reason, a portion of his letter concerning the Guild " Saint Joan " is of interest:

" The pictures have arrived. . . . On the whole there is nothing to complain of, which is a pity, as I complain so well. However lots of things are wrong; so here goes.

" In Act I the steward should be much older than Baudricourt; and both Baudricourt and Poulengy should be in half armor and be obviously soldiers and not merchants. This is important, as it strikes the note of France in war time. As it is, Poulengy's coat should not be belted. Baudricourt should be smart, a *beau sabreur*. The steward should not be a zany, but a respectable elderly man whom nobody nowadays would dream of assaulting. Otherwise B's handling of him becomes mere knockabout farce.

"In the second act Joan's hair should be bobbed; and she should be dressed as a soldier, quite definitely masculine in contrast to her girlish appearance in the first act. And at the end of the act she should be in front of all the rest, in command of the stage in the good old fashioned way from the point of view of the audience, and not beautifully composed in the middle of the picture with all the other people turning their backs to the spectators. Why don't you carry out my directions and get my effects instead of working for pictorial effects? As to the Dauphin I believe his wig is wrong. His portrait shows that his hair was completely concealed by the fashion of the time, giving him a curiously starved and bald appearance that would be very effective on the stage.

"The Bishop looks about right for the Inquisitor and the Inquisitor for the Bishop. My effect of a very mild and silvery Inquisitor and a rather stern Bishop has been missed as far as the make-up is concerned. The altar and candles in the middle of the cathedral scene are feebly stagy, and do not give the effect of a corner of a gigantic cathedral as my notion of one big pillar would. And it leads to that upstage effect, with a very feminine operatic looking Joan in the centre, which I wanted to avoid. The drag toward the conventional is very evident, and is the last word in operatic artificiality (an angry woman tears a thing downward and throws it on the floor); but still, it is all very pretty in the American way, and might have been worse."

Another letter of his concerning this play is characteristic. It was in reply to Miss Helburn's information that the Guild was using the French pronunciation of "Rheims" and also of "Dauphin":

"Terry dear, you know but little of the world.
The population of New York City is 5,620,048. The odd 48 know that the French call Rheims Rah'ce, and themselves call it variously Rance, Ranks, Rangs, Wrongs, Rass or Rams. The other 5,620,000 wonder what the 48 are trying to say, and call it Reems.

The 48 also call the Dauphin the Dough-fang or the Doo-fong.
The public laughs, and writes to me about it.
The 48 call Agincourt (an English word unknown in France) Adj Ann Coor.
You had better do what I tell you every time, because I am older than you — at least my fancy pictures you younger, and very beautiful."

The production of Ernest Vadja's Hungarian play, "Fata Morgana," directed, like "Saint Joan," by Mr. Moeller, and with middle-Europe interiors of quaint charm by Mr. Simonson, followed in March, and it, too, caught the public fancy, running for 249 performances at the Garrick and the Lyceum. The final production of the season was a re-creation by Mr. Simonson of the impressions he had received in Germany at the production there of Toller's "Masse Mensch." The tossing hands, the white arms streaming, the pictorial beauty and suggestiveness of revolutionary crowds, surging toward a fiery figure in high relief above them, were there. But in our alien and prosperous town the underlying stab of imminent reality could not be there. The play lasted for only 32 performances, and the season ended only 40 per cent successful — or less than that, if you count the production, made for subscribers only at certain matinees, of a play called "The Race with the Shadow," translated from the German, and never attempted in the evening bills.

It was said at the time that only one play out of six or even seven succeeded in the commercial theatre. The Guild had picked two out of six. But those two had to carry the Garrick Theatre, pay interest on $600,000 of indebtedness, and furnish a working capital. Only the 12,000 subscribers, who were numerous enough now greatly to reduce the losses on a failure, kept the Guild going. Even so, they entered the season of 1924–25 with just $1,000 of free funds to operate with. They were sailing about as close to the wind as it is possible to point.

But they knew where they were going; they had a definite goal in sight again, or rather two goals — the new playhouse and the acting company. Lee Simonson was having the time of his life designing, in coöperation with the architects, just the kind of stage he wanted, and the opening production at the Garrick in the Autumn of 1924 showed that work had begun on assembling the company for that stage. This opening production was a revival of Molnar's "The Guardsman," first acted in America in 1913, under the title of "Where Ignorance is Bliss," and at that time a dire failure. The leading parts were now acted by Alfred Lunt and Lynn Fontanne (Mrs. Lunt), and the play was a glittering success. It is, of course, an actor's play, and totally lacks illusion unless acted to the hilt. But the theatre is theatre, after all, and such plays have their place. Only when they lack the glamour of fine acting are they a bore. And Lunt and Miss Fontanne supplied the fine acting. The Guild, too, was realizing that fine acting includes more than intelligence; that the great ones of the stage have always had a certain vividness of personality, a mysterious, contagious quality, which electrified their technique. Bernhardt, Jefferson, Booth, Duse — the list is long. In the Lunts the Guild discerned two players who possessed vividness as well as skill, and in adding them to the small band of Guild players, in 1924, they took a wise step forward toward building a company to compare with the stock companies of the past.

"The Guardsman" ran for 271 performances, paying many bills, but hardly making the Lunts of much further use that season. The way had not yet been found to combine financial stability with flexibility of repertoire.

While the Lunts were acting "The Guardsman" Sidney Howard's "They Knew What They Wanted" was produced, with Richard Bennett, Pauline Lord and Glenn Anders in the cast. It was a great success and later won the Pulitzer prize. It, too, had to be moved to another theatre, so that presently the Guild was filling three New York playhouses. In January 1925, came a production of John Howard Lawson's "jazz symphony of American life," called "Processional." Lawson's first expressionistic play, "Roger Bloomer," had already been shown by the

Equity Players, and failed. Since 1925 he and his group of radical playwrights have made many productions, without popular success. Yet " Processional " at the Guild ran for 95 performances. It was staged by Mr. Moeller, with George Abbott and June Walker in the leading roles, and the skill and imagination displayed in this production must have had much to do with the success of a play which seems, from other experiments, to belong to a genus foreign to our American tastes. The Guild, certainly, have not felt inclined toward further experiment in this field.

The last Garrick production before the opening of the new theatre was of Milne's " Ariadne." It was rather a stop gap, and deserved its failure.

IX

The Opening of the New Theatre

THE new Guild Theatre was opened to a crowded and expectant audience of subscribers, most of whom had helped to build it by the purchase of bonds, on April 13, 1925. There had been, of course, the last minute delays and the usual frantic efforts to get the building done on time. A play by the Guild's patron saint, G. B. S., had been chosen for the first offering, and Shaw himself had been invited to attend. His reply was that he was accustomed to closing theatres, not opening them. That play was " Caesar and Cleopatra," which had not been seen in New York since the Forbes-Robertson production.

That first audience was, of course, quite as much interested in the playhouse as the play. There is no novelty about a new theatre on Broadway as a rule. One pops up every few weeks. But this one was different. It was not a real estate speculation, but a permanent institution, built to endure, and in it theatrical history would be made. Designed by C. Howard Crane, Kenneth Franzheim and Charles H. Bettis, in consultation with Norman-Bel Geddes and Lee Simonson, it was found to embody many

The Theatre Guild

interesting features within its simple Italianate walls. The auditorium is built on a mezzanine level, reached by ample stairs, and all street and lobby noises are excluded. Under it is a large lounge and grill room, and the single balcony is slung well back so that those on the rear of the floor are not seated in a cave. The seats — of which there are about 1,000 — are spacious, and men have room for their knees. There are no boxes, and the proscenium opening bears a high ratio to the width of the auditorium. This wide proscenium opening is not framed by the usual moulded arch — the dividing wall merely comes to an end. As a result of the width, the absence of architectural moulding, and the absence of boxes, there is an increased sense of intimacy between stage and audience. Moreover, the lack of the traditional arch can give to the stage a greater flexibility in future experiments in stagecraft. Behind the scenes Mr. Simonson provided for ample room to house two or more productions. There are 90 feet of fly space, ample depth and side room, and not being enamored of any single theory of stagecraft, Simonson also provided various useful machines and a wide range of lighting equipment. Above the stage and the auditorium, the guests found club rooms for the subscribers, rehearsal rooms for the company and for the newly started Theatre Guild School,* a library, shops

---

* The Theatre Guild School was conducted for two years, the first year under the direction of Winifred Lenihan, but was then given up, not from lack of pupils but because it was found that many of the pupils came on the assumption that they would be graduated into the Guild Company, and also because the directors of the Guild could not give to it the personal attention and interest they felt a school bearing their name required.

and offices. Here, then, at last was a substantially built playhouse, without gaudiness, designed to make the audience comfortable and afford work room for an acting company in repertoire and sufficient revenue possibilities to maintain that company. No new theatre in New York for many, many years had been opened with such sound promise, and so much public good will.

Unfortunately, the Guild had the theatre — but not the company. "Caesar and Cleopatra" was almost the nearest thing to an artistic failure they had yet produced, and though it was kept on for 129 performances at the new house, which many people came to see quite as much as the play, it was not financially successful, either.

The play was staged by Mr. Moeller, in settings designed by Frederick Jones III, a young man who had shown great promise, and with costumes by Aline Bernstein of the Neighborhood Playhouse. Settings and costumes were colorful, but Shaw does not live by settings and costumes. In this play especially he lives by acting, and the more pageantry and color and the tramp of armies are introduced, the less perhaps does the Shavian bite come through. Above all, the play gains dignity and worth by the character of *Caesar*, whom Forbes-Robertson beautifully interpreted as a man who could be casual because he was great. You guessed the greatness; it was up his sleeve. For *Caesar* the Guild had picked an utterly actorial actor, who left nothing up his sleeve. His greatness was a palpable sham, and the point of the play went by the board. Nor was Miss

The Theatre Guild

Helen Hayes, since become an accomplished actress in certain roles, a happy foil. This, of course, may have been the fault of Guild direction; but hers was a kitten without claws, who would have become a still kittenish bride to Antony and squealed in pretty terror at sight of the worm. The thoroughly Shavian performance of the play was given by Henry Travers as *Britannus* — and Mr. Travers, be it noted, had acted with the Guild in many parts for years. Many of the rest foundered badly on the larger stage, in this more spacious auditorium. Something was quite evidently the matter, and the Guild knew it to be the lack of a well drilled company, trained to a variety of parts, with sharp enough personalities and ample enough style to fill the new theatre. From that date on, they concentrated upon building up such a company.

The need was felt to be the more urgent because the new theatre was designed for repertoire. But successful repertoire is impossible without a large and versatile company; it is difficult to manage when you have a long list of subscribers to seat for each new play; and its financial problems are many and serious. The Guild almost immediately found that their acquisition of a fine new playhouse was merely a first step toward their goal. The real work of building up the company and solving the other problems was yet to be done. The new house, for example, together with their other expenses, called for an annual expenditure of $90,000, and this would continue to be the case until the bonded indebtedness was discharged. It left no great margin for extravagance in experiment, but demanded, instead, that a considerable proportion of their productions be made to yield the maximum of profit. They were freely criticised in some quarters for not at once inaugurating a system of repertoire. But they were primarily concerned with the stability and permanence of their institution, now representing so large an investment of money as well as hopes, and they continued to build slowly toward their goal.

The second play in the new house was again by Shaw, a revival of " Arms and the Man," the first Shaw play ever acted in America, by Richard Mansfield. Lunt played the Mansfield role, Miss Fontanne was *Raina*, and Pedro de Cordoba, trained in the New Theatre company, was *Sergius*. Henry Travers, Ernest Cossart and Jane Wheatley, all of them players of long experience and varied training, were in other parts. The production was a sound success, so much so that it could not safely be abandoned, and was presently moved to the Garrick, to make way for Molnar's " The Glass Slipper " at the Guild, a play which if it did nothing else burdened the mail box, many of the letters being from irate subscribers who missed what the Guild had felt and striven to reproduce in the play — the beauty that may shine out of evil.

In order to seat all the subscribers at " The Glass Slipper " and then to get what public patronage they could for it, the next production, a double bill composed of Shaw's " Man of Destiny " and " Androcles and the Lion," was made at the Klaw Theatre. The Guild Theatre did not house a new play till December, when "Merchants of Glory," a satirical comedy from the French, was produced. It had a brief run, and on January 25, 1926, Franz Werfel's "Goat Song" was produced, with the Lunts and several other players whom the Guild were cherishing united in the cast. Jacob Ben-Ami directed the play, and Lee Simonson made for it some of his finest settings, which remained in three dimensional reality, and yet were enough out of reality to enhance the play's symbolism and deepen its moods. An extraordinary play, acted with flaming passion, filled with tumultuous crowds and strange with vibrant over-tones, "Goat Song" left nobody neutral. Some it perplexed, some it revolted, some it filled with excited enthusiasm. Life it certainly had. To sit through it was an adventure. The production was costly, the long cast expensive, the adventure too disturbing for the general public to enjoy. It ran but 52 performances, and the Guild lost money on it. But nonetheless it was a success, for in it they began to find their stride again, to find the actors who in the larger theatre could project a character vividly, to weld a tumultuous ensemble, to fill the eye and stir the emotions. The shell was filling up with meat.

After a rather disastrous attempt by the Guild to attract the public with Evreinoff's "The Chief Thing," with McKay Morris borrowed from Mr. Belasco for the leading part, the Lunts once more became available, to end the season in a comedy, "At Mrs. Beam's," by C. K. Munro.

Miss Jean Cadell was brought from England to play *Miss Shoe*, to be sure, but the presence of the Lunts was potent. Mr. Moeller staged the play, and it ran all Summer, fortunately for the Guild, as the season had numbered, for them, a heavy percentage of financial failures. The end of the first full season at the new house found them close to rock bottom again, after their bonded indebtedness had been met, with many of their subscribers apparently dissatisfied with the choice of plays, and the way not yet found to keep together the company which it was already plain was essential to the kind of production they wished to make. Yet, in the face of such discouragements, they stuck to their guns in the choice of plays, and announced for the first bill of the next season another drama by Werfel, " Juarez and Maximilian."

X

The First Trial of Modified Repertoire—
Its Difficulties

During the preceding season, that of 1925–26, there had been great activity in the New York theatre, and many interesting productions. A comparison of that season with the season during which the Washington Square Players issued their manifesto, or that during which the Guild was founded, shows plainly that the Guild's first purpose, to produce good plays of a kind neglected by the "commercial" theatre, could no longer serve as a major goal. The preceding Winter had witnessed George Kelley's "Craig's Wife," Patrick Kearney's "A Man's Man," "Young Woodley," Miss Le Gallienne's Ibsen revivals, the Actors' Theatre revival of "The Wild Duck," Phillip Barry's "In a Garden," O'Neill's "The Great God Brown," and a visit by the studio group of the Moscow Art Theatre. The left wing dramatists, too, had been represented by Lawson's "Nirvana" and John Dos Passos' "The Moon is a Gong." There can be no question but the Guild's success had much to do with the formation of other groups, like the Actors'

The First Ten Years

Theatre, and had given other producers courage to experiment. The Guild audience, too, could absorb more than six plays a season, and turned elsewhere with their standards fixed. On the other hand, producers like Miss Le Gallienne, who appealed largely to the young, were making new audiences for the Guild. A new sense of mutual help and creative zest was spreading among the real artists of the theatre (in distinction, of course, to the shop keepers, whom we have always with us).

It was doubly needful, therefore, that the Guild progress by the formation of a permanent company and that they find some way to extract the full financial returns from a successful play without constantly breaking that company up. Beerbohm Tree once asked, "When is a repertoire theatre not a repertoire theatre?" and answered his own riddle with, "When it is a success." The Guild's problem was further complicated by the presence now of 20,000 subscribers, who had to be seated for each production, without too great complication. A nightly alternation of plays, for example, would have been quite hopeless. During their ninth season, the Guild attempted for the first time a solution of the problem. It was not an ideal solution, but it marked a step forward, and made the season of 1926–27 one of the most important in their history.

They first engaged a nucleus of ten players as a permanent company—as large a number as they felt their resources would permit after the very lean financial year which had preceded. These ten were Helen Westley, Lynn

Fontanne, Alfred Lunt, Dudley Digges, Clare Eames, Margalo Gillmore, Earl Larimore, Philip Loeb, Edward G. Robinson and Henry Travers — the majority of them, be it noted, already familiar figures on the Guild stage. It was then proposed, by renting a second theatre, to get two productions running concurrently, and presently to add two more, which would alternate, at weekly intervals. The weekly alternation was made necessary by the presence of the subscribers, to avoid too great confusion. The alternation of four plays instead of two was felt to be necessary for two reasons; first, it was difficult to find two plays in which the company could be alternately employed to the best advantage, while with four nearly every actor could be fitted in somewhere; and, second, if the plays were a success, the runs could be much more prolonged with two theatres, doubling the financial returns. The principle of alternation, either way, was the same. Every Monday all the actors would come fresh to their parts, having played something else the week before, and presumably in the course of the season each would have played three or four roles at least. The scheme did not permit of restoring to the stage any of the past successes, and was a much modified form of repertoire. But it was nonetheless a decided move forward.

The first production, made at the Guild Theatre, of Werfel's "Juarez and Maximilian," employed Alfred Lunt as the Emperor, and Miss Eames as the Empress. The play suffered the fate of most modern chronicle history plays, in spite of a very effective production, and was not put into alternation with anything else. Instead, the second production was also made at the Guild Theatre, Shaw's "Pygmalion," with Miss Fontanne in the role Mrs. Campbell had created here and Dudley Digges acting as director. This production was at once popular, and hence the third bill was mounted at the Golden Theatre, rented on an annual lease for the purpose, and Lunt, Miss Eames and all the company not acting in "Pygmalion" appeared in Sidney Howard's bootlegger comedy, "Ned McCobb's Daughter," with Mr. Moeller directing.

This play, too, was a great popular success. It was lively, contemporaneous, American, with an underlying note of significant suggestion, and it was splendidly acted. So the next problem was to pick two more plays which could be alternated with these two, containing the right number of characters to employ the company without costly lay-offs or the engagement of extra players, and yet worthy of the Guild stamp. This was something of a Chinese puzzle, and proved at once the difficulty of alternation.

The play chosen for the Golden Theatre was a second drama by Sidney Howard, "The Silver Cord," but Miss Laura Hope Crews had to be engaged for this, among other players. The play chosen for the Guild Theatre was Jacques Copeau's stage version of "The Brothers Karamazov," which he himself was brought from Paris to direct. It was so alternated with "Pygmalion" that it came on the weeks when "Ned McCobb's Daughter" was idle, and hence could employ the services of Alfred Lunt, Miss Eames and others in the Howard play. It was a disturbingly strange and stirring drama, which demanded, and received, vivid acting. While the public did not respond in great numbers to its appeal, as was perhaps natural, it afforded the actors, especially those engaged during alternate weeks in the realistic American "Ned McCobb's Daughter," a pronounced change of atmosphere and of method. Many of them noticeably benefited by becoming more theatrical, in the good sense of that abused word — less tight, that is. Fires flared from all of them, and in the dim living room of *Feodor's* house, at midnight, while that horrible old man guzzled his fish, strange tensions were in the air.

But meanwhile Miss Crews was idle on those alternate weeks when "The Silver Cord" was not acted. To get around this difficulty, special matinees of Pirandello's "Right You Are If You Think You Are" were staged, at the Guild Theatre, and when the Garrick Theatre presently became available, on her alternate weeks Miss Crews was employed in a revival of her earlier success with the Guild, "Mr. Pim Passes By." But this, of course, could not be offered to the subscribers as a substitute for a new play, so finally, when "The Brothers Karamazov" had exhausted its drawing power, a new comedy by S. N. Behrman (the third American play of the season) was mounted at the Guild Theatre, employing the Lunts, Miss Gillmore and Mr. Larimore of the permanent company, and alternating with "Pygmalion." Finally, when the regular season was over, it ran the Summer through by itself.

In many ways, this had been the most important season in the Guild's history, though the managers were far from satisfied that they had solved their repertoire problems. They had, however, made a real beginning on a permanent company, they had given the members of that company a chance at alternate roles to keep them fresh and to provide a more varied practice, they had produced three native plays of merit (incidentally the authors, Mr. Howard and Mr. Behrman, were both graduates of Professor Baker's Workshop and hence represented the same spirit in the theatre as the Guild directors), and finally they had so managed the alternation of these plays as to extract a handsome monetary return. They were now in a financial position to enlarge their company still further, the more as during the year the number of subscribers had grown to 23,000, with every prospect of more the following year. The greatest difficulty had been in the selection of plays, to find those which could alternately employ the same casts. It seriously hampered their choice, and had, indeed, postponed the production of one or two dramas they wished to do, while, if rigidly adhered to, it would entirely prevent the production of a drama which the Guild now had in hand, and were most eager to get on the stage.

XI

*"Porgy," and the First Expansion beyond New York—
Another Letter from G. B. S.—"Strange Interlude"*

THAT drama was "Porgy," made by Mrs. Heywood from DuBose Heywood's novel of the same name. The Guild saw in this drama of negro life an opportunity for the creation of a moving and beautiful picture of folk customs, they saw how a window could be opened to give us a peep into an alien world. The play was a distinct challenge to the resources and imagination of the American theatre, and they wished to accept that challenge. But obviously a negro cast would be of small use in alternation, for there was no other negro play they cared to do.

So they produced "Porgy" for their first offering, at the Guild Theatre, October 1, 1927, with a negro cast, in sets carefully modeled by Cleon Throckmorton from observation in Charleston, and directed by Rouben Mamoulian, a young Armenian, trained in Moscow, who came from the American Opera company of Rochester to the Theatre Guild School, where he gained the Guild's confidence. He proved to be just the man for the place, and "Porgy" emerged as one of the most memorable productions not only of that season, but of many seasons on our stage. But while it was running its course for the 25,000 subscribers, what was to be done with the members of the permanent company? It was decided, after much debate, and not without many misgivings, that they should make their first production outside of New York, and play elsewhere till "Porgy" was ready to move to another house.

The Guild, this season, had organized a secondary company, headed by George Gaul and Florence Eldrige, to take a repertoire of four earlier Guild successes on a tour of the country, but it was another matter to risk the regular company in cities which might not be receptive to it. Last season, however, in answer to long repeated invitations from the Philadelphia Art Alliance, the Guild had sent its company in "Pygmalion" to that city for one week's engagement. This proved successful. Accordingly they now accepted an invitation to inaugurate a repertory season in Chicago and, as the last play of this repertory, produced "The Doctor's Dilemma" prior to the New York opening. This play, which was directed by Dudley Digges, was also taken to Baltimore before it followed "Porgy" at the Guild Theatre in November. Chicago was delighted with an opportunity to share in a Guild production, and flocked to the play, which had not been shown professionally in America since that season, before the War, when Granville Barker produced it in repertoire at Wallack's Theatre. The success of this play in Chicago, the obvious welcome awaiting the Guild outside of New York, gave the Board much to think about, and led, the next season, to a new attempt to solve the problems of repertoire, and one they had not before considered.

"The Doctor's Dilemma" ran at the Guild Theatre, after "Porgy" had been moved to another house, until the next production was ready for alternation. During this run a letter came from Shaw, which is of much interest to anybody who in future attempts the play.

"I have been for some time forgetting," he wrote, " to make a criticism of The Doctor's Dilemma production. One of my directions is that there should be a lay figure on the stage. The effect aimed at is the contrast between this ludicrous and visibly unreal simulacrum of a human creature and the living figures on the stage; a contrast which becomes poignant and acquires a ghastly irony in the death scene, where Dubedat himself becomes a lay figure.

"Now your producer has taken extraordinary pains to defeat this impression, and introduce a formidable and disastrous rival to the living actors by procuring, not a typical lay figure, but a marionette with all a marionette's intensity and persistency of expression; so that when I saw the photographs I immediately said 'Who on earth is that?', not only mistaking the simulacrum for a reality, but for a leading personality. It is as if I had prescribed a turnip ghost and you have given me the Ghost in Hamlet instead.

"A good marionette (and yours is a very good one) can play any real actor off the stage.

"Sell him by auction with this letter attached for the benefit of the Guild; and make a note for reference in future productions."

On January 9 the Guild, for the first time, produced a play by Eugene O'Neill, his massive and populous "Marco Millions," in an acting version which considerably reduced the number of supernumeraries, but left enough, in all conscience. The Guild had been taken to task before now for "neglecting" O'Neill—not, of course, that he had been exactly suppressed thereby, for all of his dramas had hitherto found producers, and some of them excellent producers. But it was felt, and quite rightly, that O'Neill wrote the kind of drama the Guild was dedicated to act, and they above all others should give him hearing. Just why the Guild had not done so before, why various negotiations had broken off before the rehearsal stage, is a story of temperaments, of those differences of opinion among artists which, perhaps quite rightly, seem matters of artistic principle at the time. At any rate, until "Marco Millions," the Guild and O'Neill had never quite managed an agreement. With it, they gave him the most sumptuous production he had yet received.

Rouben Mamoulian was the director, and Lee Simonson did the settings and innumerable costumes. The acting version called for ten different sets, many of them, like the costumes, filled with Oriental pomp and color—

which, of course, was much to Mr. Simonson's liking. But, with the tremendous cast to care for also, it was essential to keep the cost of these sets within bounds and to minimize the labor of moving and storing them when the play was put into alternation. O'Neill had in part planned for this, since several of his sets call for an identical framework. But it was necessary further to carry out the scheme of unit sets, so that the Throne Room and the deck of the Royal Junk, for instance, could both make use of the same platforms and frames. If, however, sets can be thus adapted to the various needs of one production, why not to the needs of other productions? Why not make the scenery play repertoire, as well as the company? With this in mind, Mr. Simonson so designed his sets for "Marco" that the permanent frame could be adapted to the next production ("Volpone"), thus reducing the cost alike of building scenery for that play, and of moving and storing it every week when the plays were alternated. It was only by such ingenuity that the Guild was able to produce so elaborate a play as "Marco Millions," and then alternate it with another.

Critical opinions of "Marco Millions" differed widely. Some critics found in it exalted drama; some found the satire on Babbittry humorless, belated, and gaining little by being pushed back into the Middle Ages and far Cathay. Others were slightly annoyed that Marco Polo, who was, after all, one of the world's great adventurers, should be so shabbily treated. Without doubt, the character of the

The First Ten Years

Grand Khan carries far more of the genuine O'Neill than does *Marco*, of his sense of beauty and wonder and of life's deeper values. For the reader, this character ties the play together and exalts it. Not quite that effect was gained in the Guild production; perhaps the role calls for a Booth or a Mansfield or an Irving. The public, however, found enough satisfaction for eye and ear in this massive production to make it a success, and it ran for 92 performances, alternating first with "The Doctor's Dilemma," and later with "Volpone," and in the season of 1928–29 was one of the plays taken on tour to other cities, and, oddly, one of the most successful.

On January 23, 1928, at the John Golden Theatre, a second O'Neill play was produced, the much discussed "Strange Interlude," a play in nine acts, which began at 5:30 in the afternoon, with a dinner intermission of an hour after Act 5, and then continued till 11 o'clock. This, of course, is less than the three evenings required to act "Back to Methuselah," but runs "Parsifal" a close race. It is interesting to note in this connection the following letter, written by Lawrence Langner to the Board of Managers at the time they were considering the manuscript of "Strange Interlude," as indicative of the Guild motives in producing this play.

"We now have an opportunity of making a connection with Eugene O'Neill, who is considered throughout the world as the greatest dramatist America has ever produced. Let us lay aside all personal feelings and admit that a man whose plays are being given in London, Paris, Berlin, Prague, Vienna and Moscow is unique among American dramatists, and that by doing his plays we not only honor him but we honor ourselves.

"In 'Strange Interlude' we have probably the bravest and most far-reaching dramatic experiment which has been seen in the theatre since the days of Ibsen. O'Neill's genius was never more clearly shown than in this play. O'Neill has already stated that it needs cutting and is repetitive in parts. The fact remains that it is essentially dramatic, and if the drama is ever to progress as rapidly as the novel has progressed, it will be essential to adopt the new technique which O'Neill, with his astounding genius, has shown in the theatre. There can be no possible doubt as to its tremendous importance. It is as important in relation to the drama of the future as 'A Doll's House' was in relation to the theatre before it. If I have shown some vision in the past regarding the direction of the theatre, believe me when I say that this is the next step forward in playwrighting; the poetry of the unconscious to offset the stark realism of the conscious; the science of the new psychology and the mysticism of God the Father. This play contains in it more deep knowledge of the dark corners of the human mind than anything that has ever been written before. It proclaims O'Neill the great dramatic genius of the age.

"The Guild lost nothing in artistic prestige by its courage in producing 'Back to Methuselah.' It did lose the sum of $20,000 because of the extremely expensive production. With 'Strange Interlude' the Guild should not lose anything like this, because, owing to the small scenic expense and the use of a unit set, the production expense can probably be carried without financial loss by the Theatre Guild membership. None of O'Neill's plays is as perfectly written as this play; if the Guild did it, none would be better produced. If we fail to do this great experiment, if we lack the courage and the vision, then we should forever hang our heads in shame, for we will have lost one of the greatest opportunities in our history. Indeed, the theatre being what it is today, it almost devolves upon the Guild to produce this play, as the only surviving art theatre in America, for the demise of the other art theatres, such as the Neighborhood Playhouse, places upon us the solemn responsibility of being the first to recognize the work of genius and to dare to experiment, even if it be accompanied by financial loss, if that experiment be in the direction of greatness. One thing we can never lose by such a course — our prestige and our self-respect."

It was freely predicted that the public would never stand for such a protracted entertainment. They might come for a while at 5:30, but they wouldn't return after dinner. As soon as the play was launched, and its experimental technique and subject matter became known, the Broadway wisecrackers had an elegant time. Burlesquing a play in which the characters not only address each other, but speak their inmost and even their subconscious thoughts to the circumambient ether, is an easy job. There were few to predict more than a brief success of curiosity for this production.

But the wisecrackers reckoned without Shaw's dictum — that the way to succeed is to send your audience home exhausted, with something to think about. "Strange Interlude" played six performances a week (no matinees were possible, of course), for a year and a half, without a vacant seat at any performance, even in the hottest weather, during the first few months. There has probably been no stranger and more unpredicted success in the history of our theatre. Alexander Woollcott christened it "The Abie's Irish Rose of the intelligentsia." Nor, of course, can curiosity account for this success, after the first few weeks. The play, with all its possible faults and excesses — its excessive length, for one thing, its sense sometimes of overstrain and lack of saving humor — is a profoundly earnest attempt to find a new dramatic form to express the newer psychology; it has many moments of such poignant emotion as only O'Neill, on our stage, can bring about; and it has for unifying idea the lesson that only tragedy can come from our interference with other souls in their struggle for natural fulfilment.

It is no part of this history to discuss the possible effects on future play writing of O'Neill's technique in "Strange Interlude." Some critics, waxing lyric in their enthusiasm, declared they could never again be content with the ordinary play. They found, in these asides, these verbal expressions of the subconscious, overtones which imparted a glamour and richness to the dialogue, and a meaning to the situations, ordinarily lacking. That they are, or ever were, quite lacking from the work of the masters of drama is, perhaps, debatable, as it is debatable whether any of us, in our theatregoing, would care for steady doses of such introspective analysis. But the fact remains that O'Neill has shaped a new bottle — even if the glass is sometimes cloudy — for new dramatic wine, and the Guild, under the guiding direction of Philip Moeller, set it vividly before us on the stage. The settings, by Jo Mielziner, were tasteful, unobtrusive and realistic, yet carried a mood. Production concentrated on making persuasive the technique of spoken thoughts, giving them a sharp differentiation from the dialogue proper, and bringing out the emotional values of both forms of speech. The actors spoke these thoughts, or subconscious musings, into space, while the other characters sat as it were in frozen silence, not listening at all. Audiences had no trouble in differentiating, and many of the moments of thought-speech took on a strange, eerie quality of their own. The company responded nobly to the trying demands of the play, and all forces worked together to bring the drama vividly to life.

During the Summer, Miss Fontanne left the cast, and her place was taken by Miss Judith Anderson.

"Strange Interlude," playing for only six performances a week, could of course take in considerably less money than a drama given eight times. With the expense at the Guild Theatre of laying off, on alternate weeks, the enormous cast of "Marco Millions," and the expense which would have been incurred, also, if the nine sets for "Strange Interlude" had been moved out and stored every other week, the Guild were unable to maintain repertoire at the

Golden. "Strange Interlude" ran its course uninterrupted. Here was a practical problem of repertoire management not so easy to solve in fact as in a critical article in a magazine. Had the Guild not done these two dramas by O'Neill, they could doubtless have maintained their alternate performances at both houses — and continued to be abused for neglecting O'Neill. Had they, after doing the two plays, one so thoroughly experimental, attempted to continue repertoire, they would have seriously jeopardized their financial stability and future chances of doing more such plays.

All of which seems to show that repertoire without subsidy is not an easy thing to accomplish — as Miss Le Gallienne was finding out that very season down at the 14th Street Theatre, for after a brave struggle to furnish Chekhov and Ibsen to the masses, she was conducting a drive to raise $200,000 so the work could continue.

The Guild made one more production during the season of 1927–28, postponing its sixth bill till the next Autumn. The fifth production was of a translation by Ruth Langner of Stephan Zweig's "sardonic farce" adapted from Ben Jonson's famous play, "Volpone." Again Philip Moeller was the director, and Mr. Simonson adapted his sets for "Marco" until he created a gay Italian world out of Persia and Cathay. Zweig's farce boils the Elizabethan excrescences out of the old play, concentrates its plot, ironically points up its climax to let *Mosca* get away with the swag, and adds certain characters who are rather more 20th century Teutonic in tone, perhaps, than 16th century English. Finally, the whole is designed to be played in a free, swaggering *comedia-del-arte* style, which can — and in the Guild production did — remove much of the possible offense of the situations as well as the angry venom of the satire. It became a roistering comedy, edged with malice. The public liked it, and it alternated with "Marco Millions" till hot weather, and then ran the Summer out alone.

The record of "Porgy," which set a new standard for plays about the negro race and achieved authentic beauty by a synthesis of the theatre arts, a Shaw revival, two new plays by Eugene O'Neill, one of them experimental in technique and courting popular disaster by its length, and finally "Volpone," which might be called an unacademic Elizabethan revival, was the best record, artistically, the Guild had as yet hung up. Nor did the season contain a single popular failure. Every play interested the subscribers and the public as well, so that a surplus was accumulated to take care of the interest charges for two years to come, the actors shared in the profits, and there was a comfortable margin of safety for the future, making more ambitious plans possible.

But the modified repertoire system of alternating performances week by week had been more or less shattered, in order to mount "Porgy" and "Strange Interlude." Plainly that system was far from a perfect solution of their problems, and at best promised no way to keep any past successes before the public. The Guild were still fumbling toward their goal, and while "Volpone" was running the Summer out they evolved a plan which held the possibilities for a greatly increased subscription list, gave the actors weekly alternations, restored past successes to the Guild stage, and promised better drama for several cities outside New York. The formation of that plan ended this extraordinarily successful season.

XII

*Conditions on "The Road," and the
Guild's Expansion Outside of New York*

BETWEEN the time that the young Washington Square Players had issued their manifesto and the Guild's production of "Strange Interlude," the number of theatres outside New York, housing the legitimate drama, had diminished at least 50 per cent. It was a paradox of our stage that while better plays were being constantly better produced in New York, "the Road" saw fewer and fewer plays of any sort, and in many cities of considerable population the movies reigned supreme. Believing that potential audiences for the spoken drama still existed in such places, but having little confidence in the disorganized and defeated theatre of commerce to attract them, the Guild had, during the season of 1927–28 sent out a company under concert bureau management. This company played a repertoire consisting of "Mr. Pim Passes By," "Arms and the Man," "The Silver Cord," and "The Guardsman." The concert bureau secured community guarantees wherever possible, sometimes for one performance, sometimes for the entire repertoire. The tour began at Hanover, N. H., at the Dartmouth theatre, and many engagements were played in halls rather than theatres. For the actors it was hard work. But the audiences were found. The tour lasted until the end of March, and netted a small profit — not enough to have persuaded a commercial manager that it was worth the trouble, probably, but enough to persuade the Guild that even in the smaller cities organization work and good plays could rally an audience. With this experience, and with the enthusiastic response Chicago had given to the regular company, to inspire them, the Guild Board decided to make a radical departure, beginning with the season of 1928–29, from their previous system of production. They decided greatly to enlarge their company, and to open comparatively brief subscription seasons in six cities outside New York. The company would be divided into three groups, one group remaining in New York to make the first two new productions, the other groups visiting the chosen cities, each group bringing two plays from the Guild repertoire.

The advantages of this plan seemed to be many. For one thing, it promised a way not hitherto found, to keep successful productions of past seasons before the public. It also gave to the actors in the travelling groups the advantages of weekly alternation and to some of them the pleasure of developing further parts they had acted in the past. It promised, of course, greatly to enlarge the Guild's audience, and if subscribers responded in other cities as they had in

The First Ten Years

New York, would in time give the Guild a subscription list so large that financial failure would be almost impossible. With such a guarantee, a permanent company could be supported of sufficient size to meet most of their needs, and they would be freed from one of the greatest drawbacks to any form of repertoire — the restricted choice of plays. To the chosen cities outside New York, on the other hand, it promised from four to ten weeks of excellent drama, honestly produced, to which the citizens could subscribe with confidence, and by subscribing secure the best seats at a considerable reduction. "The Road" hadn't been treated in this fashion for a long, long time. Would they, or would they not, respond?

The cities chosen for the experiment were Cleveland, Chicago, Pittsburgh, Baltimore, Philadelphia and Boston. A division of the company (which this season numbered thirty-five permanent members) headed by the Lunts started around this circuit early in September, playing "Arms and the Man" and "The Guardsman," both restored to the repertoire from past seasons. In Chicago, Philadelphia and Boston each play was to run for two weeks, in the other cities one. As soon as this group had been launched, the second was made ready, and started out with "Marco Millions" and "Volpone" in alternation. Finally, in all the cities which "Porgy" had not visited the previous Spring, that play followed as a fifth offering. When the first group reached Boston, early in December, they

The Theatre Guild

rehearsed and produced in that city "Caprice," bringing it into New York immediately thereafter.

In all of these cities a subscription list was started, exactly as in New York, with the same advantages in choice of location and reduction in price. No attempt was made to disguise the fact that "Arms and the Man" and "The Guardsman" were five years old in the Guild repertoire. The appeal was made solely on the Guild's reputation for producing interesting plays in an interesting way. If the Guild met with support, the city would hereafter be assured of a certain number of good plays, well acted, every season, for which the subscriber-supporters would have the first choice of seats. The Guild didn't pretend that they were coming as philanthropists, nor ask support on that basis.

The result of this first season on the road was, on the whole, surprisingly good. In Boston, Philadelphia and Chicago audiences were uniformly large, and in the latter city "Porgy," coming for two weeks as the fifth bill, remained eleven. In the other three cities there was neither much profit nor much loss. But, what was more important, in the six cities a subscription list, the very first season, of nearly 30,000 was secured. Since the New York subscription list has steadily grown, reaching in 1929 the great number of 30,500, the list in other cities will materially increase, also, so long as the Guild continues to function as it does now, and the time will not be far off when the Guild will have, before the season begins, an assured patronage of 100,000 people, each one representing an average of $10 paid for his seats. An advance sale of $1,000,000! Already, as the season of 1929–30 starts, there is the assurance of $600,000. Out of this sum, to be sure, six productions must be made in New York, a large company paid, and four or five productions moved about the country. Nevertheless, it is a sum sufficient to drive the wolf some little distance from the door mat, assuring to the Guild financial stability, the promise of permanence, the freedom to accomplish the best that is in them.

And it has come about through the coöperation of the despised "Road," and means a better theatre in many places outside of New York.

During the first season, when this new system was being put into operation, there is little doubt but the New York subscribers sacrificed to the rest of the country — which perhaps isn't a bad thing for a change. The Guild's sudden expansion taxed the energies and resources of all its members to the full. Not only were there the subscription cities to look after, but again a secondary repertoire company was organized and rehearsed in four past successes, to play the smaller places, and before Christmas, when it still looked as if " Strange Interlude " were going to race " Abie's Irish Rose " for the long run record, a second company was specially assembled and sent out on a tour to the Coast. It was inevitable, therefore, that less undivided energy could go into the new productions made in New York, and perhaps inevitable, also, that the permanent company was not yet rich enough in talents and personalities to stand dilution into three parts. With several of its most vivid players on the road, there was certainly a tameness about "Faust," which was the first offering at the Guild Theatre in the Autumn of 1928.

The Guild had long cherished the ambition to mount "Faust" (Part 1), and had several times promised it in the past. But when it finally reached their stage, it was a distinct disappointment. Perhaps the fault was not entirely theirs. What is greatest in "Faust" is certainly not its dramatic fable, which has worn pitifully thin with the years. Moreover, they imported, to direct the play, Friedrich Holl, from the Volksbuhne Theatre in Berlin. Herr Holl had made a recent production of "Faust" in his theatre, which had attracted much attention because it removed the "operatic" elements which have crept into most performances of the old play. In Berlin Herr Holl was working with German actors, for a German audience, and may very easily have created folk pictures impossible of realization or appreciation here. The "operatic" elements, so called, in traditional performances of "Faust" represent, after all, an instinctive attempt to supply on the stage some equivalent for the lyric glory and the philosophical meditation of the printed poem, an attempt to elevate the poor little fable into the universal as the poem does. Outside of Germany they are probably inevitable, and the shade of Henry Irving would have been a better director for the Guild's revival than Herr Holl. At any rate, the public would have none of the play, and a great deal of effort and expense went for naught. One can only hope that the experience has not discouraged the Guild from any further experiment with the classics, for an occasional revival of some great work of the past, played to bring out its timeless elements, would enrich their repertory and increase their public usefulness.

"Faust," as soon as the subscribers had seen it, was followed by "Major Barbara." Mr. Moeller, who staged the Shaw revival, had already rehearsed eight plays for the road. That may have accounted for the fact that the production broke up into set speeches, as many of Shaw's plays have a perilous way of doing unless the greatest care is taken. It was not till the third production of the season, made at the Martin Beck Theatre, that the Guild struck its old stride in New York. The play was unusual—"Wings Over Europe," by Robert Nichols and Maurice Browne, and the direction by Rouben Mamoulian, who directed "Porgy," was all that could be asked.

At the end of December "Caprice" came down from Boston to the Guild Theatre, and as "Major Barbara" still had some life in it, it was moved to the Republic. So, at the start of the year 1929, not quite ten years after they made their first tentative production at the Garrick Theatre on hope and a shoe string, the Guild had four plays running in New York and seven on the road. And every one of these plays was worth seeing. There have been many managers in our history who have had eleven plays running at the same time, or even more. But none, it is safe to say, has ever upheld so high a standard uniformly in his entire product, because none has ever combined the Guild's devotion to the theatre for its own sake with such production ability and business sagacity.

Many years ago Matthew Arnold said, "The theatre is a great force in the community. Let us organize the theatre." The Guild have done it. They have organized the theatre by making the audiences their partners.

To finish the record of the season, it should be stated that three more productions were made in New York, "Dynamo," by Eugene O'Neill at the Martin Beck Theatre, "Man's Estate," by Beatrice Blackmar and Bruce Gould at the Biltmore Theatre, and finally "The Camel Through the Needle's Eye," from the Hungarian of Frantisek Langer, a comedy which ultimately ran the Summer out at the Guild Theatre. Finally, early in the Spring the "Porgy" company was taken to London where the play and, still more, the production were warmly received by the critics, though the public was more apathetic: and later Mr. Lunt and Miss Fontanne, with the "Caprice" cast and production, journeyed to the same capital, which since James H. Hackett made his first trip there almost exactly a century ago has been a goal of New World players. "Caprice" was still highly popular in New York when its run was broken for the London trip, and that expedition was really a vacation and reward to the Lunts for their brilliant contribution to the success of the Guild, and their devotion to its company and ideals in the face of numerous temptations from other managers and the " speakies."

O'Neill's " Dynamo " was a distinct disappointment. Announced as the first of a trilogy which was to struggle dramatically with the problem of religion in our new machine age, it persuaded many people that as a leader of religious thought O'Neill is a splendid writer of melodrama, and caused at least one Guild subscriber to write that he would renew his subscription only on condition that the remaining plays of the trilogy were not produced. It employed the " Strange Interlude " technique of spoken thoughts but seemed to gain little by the method. The settings by Simonson, especially that showing the interior of a power house, were more striking than the play. " Man's Estate," the other American drama of the season, was rather too trite and simple-minded for a successful Guild offering. " The Camel Through the Needle's Eye," like " Caprice," was Middle European comedy done with a certain style and air, but of small intrinsic importance. Actually, the season was notable only for " Wings Over Europe," for the silken production " Caprice," and for the organization of the new road tour.

Punch, commenting on " Caprice " in its issue of June 12, 1929, remarked:

" This seems to be the best presentation of a comedy in English on the English stage since the Barker-Vedrenne association at the Court Theatre. . . . A presentation and performance distinguished in its parts and even more

The Theatre Guild

distinguished as a whole. It has, in a word, the rare quality of style and exquisite balance. . . . The New York Guild . . . have laid us under a deep debt of gratitude, and those lovers of the theatre who have eyes to see can read a lesson in this performance. This finish, this balance, this style are the result of hard work by a patiently organized, stable group of actors, producers and (not less important) theatre-goers inspired by an artistic ideal. The New York Theatre Guild has twenty-four thousand subscribing members, which is to say that New York theatre-goers of intelligence have determined to back their best players and producers instead of leaving them to the mercies of the gambling entrepreneurs and rack-renters who have the London theatre in their grip and who more than any other cause are responsible for its present unhappy condition."

And this from Punch about something American! The case could hardly be better stated, though Punch could not know that still more significant was the fact that "Caprice" was produced in Boston first, where there are now 7,000 subscribers, and it represents not the organization of intelligent theatregoers in New York alone, but in half a dozen cities of the United States. That expansion of the Guild organization in 1928–29 from New York to take in a much larger territory, and one which much more than New York needed such ministrations, was of course the real work of the year, and its success may well excuse a temporary lapse in standard for some of the new plays and productions.

XIII

What About the Future?

THE Guild entered the season of 1929–30, its eleventh year, with its company still further enlarged by the engagement of Alice Brady, Frank Conroy, Alexander Kirkland and several other players, so that each group into which the company might be divided would have its share of vivid actors. The acting company, in addition to these recruits, now numbered the following: Glenn Anders, Elliot Cabot, Morris Carnowski, Ernest Cossart, Dudley Digges, Lynne Fontanne, George Gaul, Earl Larimore, Philip Leigh, Alfred Lunt, Douglas Montgomery, Tom Powers, Claude Raines, Elizabeth Risdon, Gale Sondergaard, Henry Travers and Helen Westley. Washington, Detroit, Cincinnati and St. Louis were added to the six cities already on the subscription circuit (Boston, Baltimore, Philadelphia, Pittsburgh, Chicago and Cleveland), and to these ten cities it was planned to send "Strange Interlude," "Wings Over Europe," "Major Barbara," "Pygmalion" and "Caprice," as well as "Marco Millions," "Volpone" and "R. U. R." to those cities where the latter three plays have not already been seen. A travelling repertory company which, the year before, had through local coöperation established something like a subscription season in many other cities was reorganized as a part of the regular company, and will present "Marco Millions," "Volpone" and "R. U. R." The Capek drama, one of the Guild's most interesting earlier productions, was thus restored to the stage. The company of "Porgy" will also make an extensive tour to the Pacific Coast after having achieved an uninterrupted engagement of nearly two solid years, divided between New York, the eastern American cities and London. Already half the Guild subscribers are outside of New York; and half the year many of the Guild actors spend beyond Broadway. And that is as it should be.

For lay the blame as you like on movies and motors and radios and what-not rival distractions, what has alienated many thousands of theatregoers from their ancient playhouses through the land has been loss of confidence in the value of the stage entertainment sent to them by the shopkeepers of Broadway. Lacking the creative energy and resources to rebuild for themselves local playhouses to take the place of the old local stock companies, which the shopkeepers had destroyed, these people have long been without a theatre worthy of the name. The welcome accorded to the Guild Company in Boston, Chicago and elsewhere was a vote of confidence. The Guild standards of play selection, acting and production were known. The Guild's method of subscription seats was fair and reasonable and never discriminated against people of moderate means. It was noticeable the very first season that the subscribers in other cities, as in New York, very soon assumed a kind of proprietary air; they became a part of this movement, this theatre which was coming to them. It wasn't the same thing to Boston, of course, that the old Museum had been, nor to Philadelphia what Mrs. Drew's company had meant. But it was the nearest to them these cities had known in a long time. Here was a season of plays they could attend with perfect confidence, seeing the same actors in at least two roles, learning to know and to like them, and assured that the experience they were going through as each play unfolded was as rich and significant as the American stage of today can offer.

When, in September, 1929, the Guild fell foul of the ridiculous Boston censorship, and the Mayor refused to permit a showing of "Strange Interlude," the Guild subscribers rallied almost to a man in support of the play. It was shown in Quincy, on September 30, and the subscribers, with some thousands of other Bostonians, journeyed cheerfully out to see it, and gave its cast seventeen curtain calls on the opening night. Incidentally, investigation showed that neither John Adams nor John Quincy, his son, had turned in his grave.

Moreover, when the Guild company departed from these cities it left behind this body of subscribers more keenly receptive than they had been to theatrical enjoyment. Theatregoing is a good bit of habit, and one easily lost under continued disappointment. There is plentiful evidence in New York that the great body of Guild subscribers there make up a not inconsiderable part of the audiences for the offerings of other artistic managers — that there is action and reaction. The increasing body of Guild subscribers in its subscription cities beyond New York will more and more become an audience for other plays of assured merit, or for local creative efforts which can demonstrate their worth. Ultimately, indeed, these people may demand a theatre of their own, and we shall round the circle back to the local stock companies of old. But meanwhile the Guild is a local stock company, as it were, to eleven cities now, on part time in all but New York. It has realized, through hard experience, that the theatre cannot reach its best estate except it gather and train a permanent company; that this company must be large in order to permit a free choice of plays and make possible any alternation; and that to support such a company, without a subsidy, a large population must be tapped.

The Guild have gathered such a company now, and in numerous instances, such as "Caprice," have brilliantly demonstrated what it can do. By their road season they have found the way to tap a large population, at the same time bringing great benefits to that population, and a way also to give their actors a chance at alternate roles and to restore past plays to the repertoire. One problem, however, they have not yet worked out satisfactorily — that of playing repertoire in New York, where they are obligated to make six new productions a season for nearly 34,000 subscribers. With so many subscribers, this cannot possibly be accomplished in repertoire in a single playhouse. It will be necessary for the Guild to rent one and perhaps two additional theatres, even to put plays into weekly alternation in New York, without any attempt to keep older plays on view. Actually, no doubt, they ought to own another well-equipped house on Broadway. Perhaps that will come in time. At any rate, their goal of genuine repertoire in New York is as yet unattained, and they have a major objective still to strive for.

Financial stability they would seem to have achieved, by the steady increase of subscribers till a million dollar advance sale is a possibility in the near future. The six Managers who constitute the Guild, as we have before stated, do not share in the increased earnings of the organization proportionately to that increase. Only two or three years ago one of them figured that in the first seven years of the Guild the average income of each Manager, from the theatre, was less than $3,000. It is more now, but not proportionate to the increased income of the organization. By the terms of the indenture under which the bonds were sold, half the profits go to retiring these bonds, and the other half is accumulated for reserve needs. In 1929, for example, $80,000 worth of bonds were retired. The Guild has never paid a dividend. Had the six men and women who constitute it been actuated by the love of gain, neither severally nor collectively would they have stuck out the years of struggle nor built up the extraordinary going concern they now administer. They were actuated, severally and collectively, by a love of the theatre and a passion to make this child of theirs a worthy and enduring thing.

That, of course, has been their great strength; but it is also, in a sense, their weakness. For, in closing this account of an organization which means so much now to our American theatre, which is so carefully observed by all other groups striving to create a worthy playhouse, we cannot refrain from saying that the Guild have builded something which in a real sense belongs to the public. By their very unselfishness and refusal to use their success for self-exploitation, they have become public servants. Therefore, the perpetuation of the Guild when the six who now constitute it have laid down the reins of management becomes a matter of public interest. These six, after trial and error, have functioned as a committee when everybody said you couldn't run a theatre that way. They have admitted others to their membership, only to learn that the combination wasn't right. None of them is yet old, or even elderly. But they aren't as young as they were in 1919, and sooner or later they will have to face the necessity of finding a way to perpetuate their work, or else see it discontinued.

At the present moment, it is perhaps doubtful if any one of them has given the matter much thought, since the problem is happily not immediate and they have been busy with problems of the hour. But by organizing the disorganized and discouraged audiences of New York and other cities, by building up an acting company, by creating, with public aid, a comfortable, well-equipped, permanent playhouse amid the stucco shacks of Broadway, and by establishing a tradition of fine drama, forward-looking and alert, they have laid the foundations of what might, and surely should be, an enduring institution larger than the individuals who have created it, as a university is larger than its founders. Self-supporting, unendowed, the tool of no government, nor cult, nor patron, it should be passed on to the future as the finest monument its creators could desire. Just how that is to be accomplished it is difficult even to surmise. We shall have to leave the problem for the Board of Managers to thrash out in one of their Sunday night meetings, where, as you may read in their own accounts, so many of their problems have simmered and boiled till the solution came to the surface.

BEHIND THE SCENES WITH THE EXECUTIVE DIRECTOR

By Theresa Helburn

I REMEMBER an emergency meeting of the Board of Managers of the Guild called one Monday afternoon nine years ago in the dim, dirty attic of the Garrick Theatre, which, with a few partitions at one end, served as office, rehearsal and Board room for the infant Guild. Langner, Moeller, Simonson, Wertheim and Helen Westley were at that time, owing to a recent upheaval, the only members of the Board. I was there by courtesy, as I had been for the last three months. Although I was officially only the "Play Representative," I had from the beginning been an intimate member of the Guild group. I particularly remember the gloom of the big, bare room, the uncomfortableness of the rickety chairs, and the general feeling of *malaise* that prevailed at the meeting. Rollo Peters, the original executive, and Augustin Duncan, the only real professional of the group, had resigned. The five remaining members had "gone to the mat" over the question of group or individual control. It had left them triumphant, but disorganized and considerably worried by their victory. They had no executive and no stage director, for Moeller was still too close to his amateur standing and too much a part of the group to be recognized as a savior by his own people. Simonson, who had been acting executive since Peters' resignation — a job for which he was ill-fitted, both by temperament and inclination — had somewhat explosively resigned, and the business manager, a handsome and strong-minded young woman, was on the point of following suit. This seemed like the ultimate disaster, for who was left? Various possibilities for a new executive were under consideration, but meanwhile the business of the theatre must go on.

At midnight, the night before, I had written Finis to a three-act play and I was still in that state of blissful elation which for a brief moment follows any creative work. Therefore I came rashly to the breach and offered to carry on the executive work as best I could during the interregnum. It was a doubtful offer for I knew nothing of the business of the theatre, my sole experience having been in writing plays and watching production; but I understood the temper of my colleagues, was in complete sympathy with their point of view, and I was, after all, the only available straw to clutch at — a frail support, but, we all thought, a temporary one. In a few weeks one of our more experienced candidates would, we felt sure, be ready to "take over." In any case the business manager, whose feelings had been ruffled, would now stay on and help hold the fort. But we had reckoned without the temperament of the lady, who was also an actress in her off hours. A new crisis immediately arose. As soon as the upstart executive began to exercise authority for the Board, she was given to understand that certain matters were under the jurisdiction of the business manager, and not to be questioned. It was, on a smaller scale, the same issue which had caused the resignation of the two members from the Board — the desire for autocracy on the part of one person more experienced, perhaps, than the others. To this problem there was only one answer. As soon as the group realized the lady's objection was not to one particular executive, but to any executive, her resignation was forced and I found myself the acting head of a theatre with no experience and little or no counsel to guide me. For both Mr. Langner and Mr. Wertheim, on whom I counted most for practical advice, were called away on protracted trips at this crucial moment. I doubt whether any one ever learned as much about the theatre in so short a time as from sheer necessity I did in that first month. For the two weeks were lengthened into four and then, as the other candidates were found unavailable, further protracted, until finally I was taken formally into the Board of Managers and made Executive Director instead of Executive Secretary pro tem.

There are several interesting angles to this final decision of the Board and its bearing on the history of the Guild. In the first place, I was perhaps more of an amateur than any of my colleagues, and my inexperience made me not only agreeable to, but dependent on the group system of government. And necessity, as well as desire, soon taught me how to get the greatest amount of coöperation from my colleagues. Second, my interest in and previous experience of the theatre had been entirely from a creative and artistic angle. I had never looked upon the theatre as a business, and though I had, willy-nilly, to learn this business, it always occupied in my mind a place of secondary importance. It was the necessary and unavoidable means to an end, that end being production; it was never the purpose for which production was carried on. This mirrored the underlying attitude of my five associates, for whom the Guild was a gesture of artistic experiment and to whom the idea of profit seemed in those early years both fantastic and beside the point. I was therefore tuned to the right key to voice the sentiments and execute the decisions of the Board of which I was a member, even when from a strictly business point of view these decisions seemed impractical and extravagant. Indeed, as I look back, I seem to have frequently found myself gently apologizing to our business manager for decisions that appeared to thwart the logical and successful development of his department. And it takes as much tact to persuade a good business manager to sacrifice immediate profit for a vague and uncertain artistic end as to convince an impassioned stage director that you can't pay a star's salary to the actor who has six lines

The Theatre Guild

in Act I, or an inspired scenic artist that imagination must be limited by the expense of the stage crew. Sometimes arguing on one side of the fence, sometimes on the other, the executive of an art theatre must be constantly ready to shift points of view and methods of attack.

And this brings me to the third point of my relation to the Guild and to my job. This ability to see both sides of the case, this willingness to help bring about the inevitable compromises between the various elements in the theatre can, I think, only be successfully maintained when the executive has no direct personal end at stake. And I would stress it as an important point in the formation of all group organizations of this sort that the executive be not involved as actor, director, designer, nor in any other definitely creative role.

It was undoubtedly lucky for me that the tradition of not producing plays written by ourselves had been established to lessen unavoidable conflicts between our artistic egos and our managerial roles. Other members of the Board went through the fire and learned to make the inevitable sacrifices, and I must say that no one ever failed to accept the personal defeat without rancor. It has always been the Guild first — never the person. This was the unwritten law to which everyone had to submit or go his individual way.

It must be understood that the six directors of the Guild are none of them figureheads. It is not a matter of an occasional meeting and a few words of advice. There is, to begin with, the constant duty of play reading, for all plays are chosen for production by a majority vote of the Board. The material has, of course, to be first weeded out by the play readers, and, owing to direct contacts with authors and agents, the executive cannot avoid reading a preponderant number of manuscripts. Yet each member of the Board reads probably one or two plays a week, and often more. It is indeed one of my constant and most difficult tasks to see that no member ever has the privilege of retiring peacefully without an unread manuscript on his or her bed-table — an inescapable temptation or irritant, as the case may be. This is the first and most sacred duty of Board members. Second, and no less sacred, is attendance at what are known as managers' rehearsals — special complete run-throughs of every play, held usually on Sundays, two weeks and one week before the opening night. These rehearsals are, I believe, known to the actors as the " death watch," for it is no easy ordeal to run through a play only half learned and partially rehearsed before an audience of critics only; an audience, moreover, of six people already familiar with the material, impervious to the stimulus of suspense, sitting silent and apparently unresponsive, pencil in hand, flashing electric torches or cigar lighters every now and then in the darkened auditorium in order to indulge in the menace of a critical note. Nevertheless these rehearsals, harrowing as they may seem to the company, and burdensome often to the managers themselves, who might be spending a quiet Sunday in the bosom of their family or holding high revel with friends, have proved of incalculable value to the development of the Guild.

Production is never, in my opinion, a one-man job, for the director himself grows inevitably so close to a play in the repetitive routine of rehearsals that he loses perspective. In the careful building up of detail and atmosphere he may sometimes lose sight of the larger issues at stake, or, obsessed by some sweeping idea, he may neglect essential minutiae entirely. No one is proof against the danger. I have seen the finest directors guilty of the strangest lapses. I remember, for example, a manager's rehearsal of a certain tragedy that seemed to us, although it was a full week before opening, already nearly perfect in characterization, detail of action, pace, etc., until it came to the final scene — a death scene which should have been the climax of the play — and this was handled with such extreme delicacy that none of us could tell whether the heroine had died from poison, as the author, we thought, intended, or just casually dropped off in a faint, tired by the preceding emotional scene. I remember the Board hurrying on the stage at the end of the play for the inevitable conference with the director.

"But, good heavens!" we cried, "Does she die — or doesn't she?"

"Why stress the point?" said the director, suavely. "Why not let the audience take it as they will?"

"But she dies," we protested. "We know she dies. We've read the play."

The First Ten Years

"Need we make the ending so pointedly unpleasant?" said the director.

The vote on this point was most emphatically "yes," and the final week was devoted by the reluctant but compliant *regisseur* to building up a poignantly beautiful death scene that proved, as it should have, the high spot of the play. I hate to think what the reaction would have been on the first night had the audience witnessed the vague sentimentality of that earlier ending.

I can recall a managers' rehearsal at which the director's whole attack seemed to us wrong and had to be shifted; another at which an important character was entirely misinterpreted; others at which there was no tempo and no variety; one where the action, grouping and interplay were amazing, and no attention given to the reading of lines; and so on. There are innumerable stops to be played in the symphony of production and any one of them may be neglected or forgotten by a director in his intense concentration on something else.

Perhaps the most magic moment in the theatre is that when the house lights are first dimmed, the footlights go up, and the audience sits in hushed anticipation for a moment before the curtain actually rises. Battered and sophisticated theatre-goer as I am, I never fail to respond to this matchless second when hope lifts its wings from the ashes of past disappointments. And to me the most vital moments in our experiences before production are the ones that follow close on the heels of a managers' run-through.

The Theatre Guild

The stage manager bangs his little table with his fist and cries "Curtain," for there is no scenery or crew or actual rise and fall of a real curtain at these rehearsals to help the illusion. Gradually the six of us shift from our cramped positions, feel in the dark aisles for lost possessions, and climb the rickety stairs to the stage. The company is greeted and hurried off home as quickly as is politely possible; and then the managers, the stage director and the unfortunate author, if he happens to be alive and in the country, settle down around an improvised table. There is a moment's pause; then each in turn says his say — this actor is miscast; that scene is misplayed; the beginning of the act is too long; the end is too weak; there is too much action, or too little; these values are not realized, those are over-stressed. It is surprising how many things can be wrong with what might seem to an outsider an exceedingly good rehearsal.

To the director or author new to our method the first experience comes as a difficult ordeal, for we are so concerned with getting faults made right that we entirely forget to mention the already existing virtues, and our convictions are so intense that when opinions disagree the battle often becomes violent. But ultimately the director realizes that though we may criticize, we never blame; that no one's is the fault, but every one's the responsibility. For we know that destructive criticism is death to the morale and spirit of rehearsal, and so we allow ourselves to think only in constructive terms. And the director, having passed through the fire, finds that he has been immensely stimulated by it, indeed — for all its fury — warmed and cheered. He has had the preliminary reactions of an audience. For the first time his play has lived, and often he is the first to recognize the weaknesses of this premature birth. At the second showing the child will be infinitely stronger, better balanced, more articulate; and after this second showing, a week later, there will be a further conference of the powers to help the infant, if possible, to a long life and a brilliant one.

Often, of course, it is not the director, but the author, who is at fault — especially if it is a hitherto untried play — and then the conference turns to the discussion of revisions, sometimes agreed on then and there, sometimes delegated to the author or director or to these two in conjunction, if necessary, with one or two members of the Board. Not using the Broadway system of preliminary try-outs, the managers of the Guild have had to constitute themselves their own one-night stand. We are "the dog" on which the author may — indeed, must — try his wares and prove them palatable, and we have found that as try-out dogs we are much nearer the temper and taste of the ultimate New York pack than any small-town audience would be.

I have dealt at length with this system of managers' rehearsals for it is the keystone of our production arch, and I think we owe to it the high majority of our successes over our failures — a ratio considerably higher than the average. Of course, dress rehearsals are important, too, but they are not all of them compulsory on the entire Board. But compulsory managers' rehearsals are held not alone for each new production but for each re-produced play that goes on tour, so that at certain times of the year this business of being a manager of the Guild becomes much more exacting than being a mere banker or lawyer or artist or husband or wife or parent, as the case may be.

Furthermore, the Board of Managers meets in executive session once a week, usually on Sunday evenings, for when Miss Westley is acting (and when isn't she?) it is her only free day. Frequently Sunday afternoons, therefore, have to be given up to rehearsals and Sunday evenings to meetings — for weekday afternoon sessions not only cut too deeply into business hours, but are apt to be brief and interrupted. We have found it important that these weekly meetings should be as long and as leisurely as possible. For that reason we have formed the habit of dining at each other's houses and fortifying ourselves in advance by an excellent meal. Indeed, the care with which these dinners are ordered has become not only a matter of rivalry, but who knows what amount of log rolling for some pet policy has been accomplished by an excellent roast or a particularly good soup!

There is no formality about the meetings, no attempt to conduct them according to parliamentary or any other law. There is no stenographer present, for that would destroy their freedom and intimacy, and whatever notes are taken are jotted down hastily by the executive. But I may as well confess that participation in a discussion is so much more important than recording it that the minutes are, I fear, dictated almost entirely from memory the following morning. From time to time various members of the staff join the meetings for discussions or reports on their particular problems, most often, of course, our invaluable business manager, Warren Munsell. Occasionally it seems advisable to have our press representative or a play reader or some one from another department come to a meeting for a short time in order to keep fresh the contact between the department heads and the Board as a whole. But the best part of the meetings is those rare times when the actual business is over and we sit around the fire with still time and energy left to go on talking. Those are the moments when we ask ourselves what next, when we look back and draw conclusions, when we look ahead and dream. Then everyone talks of his or her pet play or pet project and what they would like to see the next years bring forth, and like as not it all ends in talk — and like as not again the seed of one particular idea takes root in several other minds and germinates, so that the next time it comes up for discussion the ground is prepared and the seed very likely to bear fruit.

For this reason it is almost impossible to analyze the different contributions of the various members of the Board. Though each one may have his separate functions, and the actual running of the organization and work of production falls most heavily on two or three, we are all concerned with the formation and development of policy and plan. And I would suggest that another plank in the formation of all art theatres be, that a certain number of meetings be set aside for the discussion of no business whatsoever; that these meetings be held not around a table, unless it be a dining-table, but around a fire, or on a terrace overlooking quiet water, or in any place conducive to the atmosphere of leisure, rare enough in America and practically nonexistent in the American theatre. For it is in these moments that the really creative ideas of our theatre have been born.

Discussions of plays form, naturally, a very important part of these weekly Board meetings, and the constant variety of opinion in these discussions is as surprising as it is valuable. Surprising because over a period of ten years there seems to have been no regularity of reaction, no cliques, no assurance that certain groups will think alike. A play is bought on a vote of four or more; on a vote of three to three, it is stalled and sometimes brought up for reconsideration again and again by its supporters if they are sufficiently enthusiastic. This enthusiasm may ultimately win an exhausted concession from the opposing faction and result in a production, but this has usually proved itself an unwise procedure. Not only is it hard to undertake the uphill task of production without more concerted eagerness to start the ball rolling, but results have more often than not proved these divided choices unwise ones. For as at rehearsals, so also in play reading, the six of us represent an audience in miniature; an audience, it is true, of specialists in the theatre, but as varied in temperament and reaction as any half-dozen ticket-holders chosen at random from their seats on an opening night. If the majority of our Board sincerely and enthusiastically like a play and think it worth producing, then there is a pretty good chance that the majority of our audience will feel the same way. If we are divided among ourselves, there is apt to be a similar uncertainty and division in the minds of the public. This pre-gauging of audience reactions is another important contribution of group organization to our development.

It has often been said that a theatre can be run successfully only by an autocrat, and there may be some truth in the theory provided that the autocrat is a genius. Failing the genius, give me six good theatrical minds working together for a common end. The sum of the six is very apt at times to approximate that of the genius and their varied contribution is worth more than any discipline or organization that mere autocracy can give.

It is, however, time for me to mention that, surprising as it may seem under the circumstances, the Guild has developed an extremely efficient organization. It was certainly not developed by autocracy. Perhaps the very inexperience of the executive may have had something to do with it, for with my limited theatrical background I could not take in raw material and train it myself; neither, on the other hand, could we afford experts. It followed, therefore, that my subordinates had to learn their jobs along with me and sink or swim as the case might be. As, however, they had only one job to learn, while I had many — and in addition the major burden of casting had fallen on my shoulders — it seemed fair to expect that they should not only keep pace with, but surpass, their superior officer. Having unexpectedly started at the top of the business instead of working my way up from the bottom according to approved theory, I have never been in the position of knowing the theatre from the ground up and of being able to boast that I knew more about all its branches than my technical assistants. Indeed, I very soon learned that if a department head couldn't teach me about his department he did not belong in the Guild. It has proved, of course, not only an acid test, but a strong spur to the newcomers in the organization, and it is surprising how quickly and efficiently comparatively untrained people developed under the stimulus of real responsibility and the new adventure.

At this point I must pause to register our profound debt to Warren Munsell, Business Manager of the Guild. Formerly with the Washington Square Players, he came into the Guild a year after my assumption of the executive role, and soon proved himself an invaluable addition to our staff. We found ourselves indebted not only to his business experience in the theatre, but to the quiet assurance with which he met and mastered the new business problems that were forever confronting us. Moreover, his understanding and exploitation of new opportunities as they opened before us, had much to do with the successful enlargement of the Guild's program. To me, he has proved not only an unfailing staff on which to lean, but the most serene and understanding of colleagues.

There are, I suppose, five departments in most producing theatres, and six in a subscription theatre like ours: the production, the play reading, the technical, the publicity, the business and the subscription departments.

Our subscription department is an outgrowth of the business department, under whose jurisdiction it remains. It has long been headed by Miss Addie Williams whose skillful tact and vital personality have done much to maintain the cordial relations which exist between the Guild and its members. The business department is at present concerned with the leasing and running of all theatres, with the supervision of accounts, the control of all box offices, making of contracts, booking of road tours, etc.; but in the early days when Mr. Munsell first joined the organization, he had a much easier time of it. In those days I was able to handle all contracts, there was but one theatre of our own and at the most two box offices to superintend, and the subscription department consisted of a few hundred names in a precious book kept in the cash drawer. I remember a message sent up from the retiring business manager to Mr. Munsell at the time of his incumbency: "Better not take any more subscriptions," it ran; "we have five hundred now and we ought to keep some seats for the public." It is an amusing anecdote, in the light of our present membership of over 30,000 in New York alone.

The growth of our subscription audience has been a

steady one and deserves some explanation, for often representatives of other art theatres have come to us seeking information concerning our subscription policy. The mistake most of them make is, I think, in seeking too much subscription support before they start to work and have something actually to show and sell their public. " He either fears his fate," etc., is essentially true of an art theatre. I remember a very pleasant gentleman from the Middle West who came to call on me a few years ago in reference to a civic theatre that was to be sponsored in his home city by a group, and more especially by one very wealthy citizen. We had just moved into our new theatre after seven years at the old Garrick and were looking at the moment, I admit, unusually new and prosperous. I showed the gentleman all over the theatre and then we returned to my office. " Well now, how did you do it? That's what I've come here to ask you," he began.

" Do what? " I asked.

" Do all this — get your subscribers? " he said, with a sweep of his hand that seemed to indicate a subscriber concealed behind every chair.

" We have been producing for eight years," I ventured.

" I know — I know all that," he said; " but how did you get your subscribers. You have 15,000. We want ten."

" But we have been producing eight years," I reiterated.

Still he failed to see the connection. " We want 10,000," he repeated, "and this is our present plan. What do you think of it? " And he proceeded to unfold an elaborate system of chain tickets, reduced rates, premiums, privileges, etc.

"But what plays are you planning to do? Who are your actors? What directors have you? What, in short, is your production plan?" I demanded, a trifle shortly, for had I been of the sex that wears collars I should have begun to feel a little hot under mine.

"Oh, that will all be attended to," he replied with a vague gesture. "What we want now is subscribers. You say you have $15,000; well, we'll be content with ten for a start."

And had we not mercifully been interrupted, he might still have been throwing that demand up against my dogged repetition of eight years of production.

Mr. Eaton elsewhere outlines the gradual growth of our subscription audience from the original 150 members to its present size, but it is interesting to note that though those years which showed the greatest number of popular successes were followed by the greatest new subscription demand, throughout our history the variation in renewals has been negligible, compared to the solid phalanx of members who stood with us through thick and thin, accepting the bad with the good, realizing that we were bound to make mistakes, but enduring these mistakes patiently for the sake of what had been and might be to come. I wonder what percentage of this audience is conscious of what an integral part of our theatre they are and have always been, of how they are the breath of life to our plays. Without them we could never have gone on producing play after play for ten years, and this quite apart from the real importance of their financial contribution. Only some one who knows the hectic agony of production can realize what it means to the producers if they are working with real conviction and intensity to know that whatever happens the play will not be still-born, that it will be given a chance of life for at least five or six weeks and that if thereafter it cannot stand on its own merits, it has at least had a decent chance from its public. I do not believe any art theatre group could persist with freshness and enthusiasm for long without this support.

As to the actual means of recruiting this subscription audience, it has been done most largely, of course, by mouth to mouth advertising, but also by the use of mailing lists, by the distribution of literature and pledge cards in the theatres, by subscription speeches from the stage — an annoying but effective method — and by occasional whirlwind campaigns in which we were greatly assisted by volunteer help from our friends. To Mr. Paul Moss, Mr. Bela Blau, Mr. Benjamin Kaye and many others we owe sincere acknowledgment for services freely and selflessly rendered.

A word or two more on our other departments. Our general financial policy will be treated elsewhere in this book. It was at Mr. Wertheim's wise insistence that we began keeping detailed accounts and weekly balance sheets long before our assets justified the trouble. This persistent and insistent knowledge of where we stood financially, while it did not enable us to make money, kept us from finding ourselves plunged into debt before we knew it, as has been the disastrous lot of many art theatres. When we were up against financial crises — and they were numerous enough in those early days — we could at least be cautious in the choice of our next production. When I say cautious, I do not mean that we could choose a play to make money; even if we had wanted to, we didn't know how, nor do we to this day. The longer any one is in the theatre, the more keenly he realizes its fortuitous quality. We have had only one system to guide us in the gamble, only one criterion in choosing a play, and that is — does it say enough to us and say it well enough to be worth the effort of production?

But one thing we could do; we could choose a play scenically simple enough to demand no great production cost or running expense. It is not always easy to find fine plays at hand demanding only one set and a few characters, but twice St. John Ervine saved our youthful and precarious existence with such fodder; first, with "John Ferguson," and again, a year later, with "Jane Clegg," a beautiful play which we managed to put on most successfully with only a few hundred dollars in the bank.

Economy has had, also, to play an important part in our scenic and technical departments; but let me say emphatically that this has been no hardship. An ounce of imagination is worth a carload of scenery, as any genuine artist in the theatre will admit. Lee Simonson did the entire production of "From Morn to Midnight," an expressionistic play in seven scenes, for $2000, and it was one of his most interesting and satisfying productions. His "Liliom" was equally simple and successful. Again and again we have found that the limitation of means has served as a stimulus rather than a hindrance to the scenic artist, just as perhaps the limitations of verse forms are a help to the poet. This doesn't mean that in these days of mounting costs you can put on any show for very little money, but we have found that in those cases where we allowed our scenic artists too lavish a hand, instead of extravagance helping the play, it has succeeded only in drowning more important values and been a contributing factor to failure.

The technical department is perhaps the most hardworked of any in the theatre, for on it falls all the last-minute strain of the hectic rush that precedes production. There is no eight-hour day in a technical department. Twenty-four hours is sometimes all too short to accomplish the varied tasks put upon its members by the demands of the director, actor, costumer, and the scenic artist. And to them falls all the blame, and, I fear, not nearly enough of the praise for a successful production. A word of sincere tribute is due to the serenity of the two technical directors who have presided over the department during the major part of our history, Carolyn Hancock and Kate Drain Lawson. Their calm and steady persistence through the storms of depression and gusts of temperament that hover

over final rehearsals has always been a matter of amazement and admiration to us all.

Our press department has had to struggle to maintain the importance of its position with probably less help from the executive than any other department. It has always been difficult for me to remember that details of production and matters of running policy were not really domestic secrets, but of interest to outsiders, and grist for the ever-hungry maw of the publicity department; and I have often found our press representatives justly complaining that they heard news of Theatre Guild activities from actors in the company or rank outsiders before I had even realized they were of sufficient importance to deserve an official *communiqué*. Perhaps this is another result of my sex, whose ideal of running a household properly is to do so without interference and with as little noise as possible. Luckily, however, the coöperation of the newspaper men, who have from our beginnings been keenly and generously interested in promoting the Guild idea and helping both by praise and criticism, has more than atoned to the press department for being neglected at home. And our unvarying policy of never sending out any statement that was not accurate and without exaggeration has sustained this cordial and fair-minded attitude of the press toward our work. Of course, when there were important publicity problems which needed careful preparation, Miss Benedict in the early days or Mr. Sisk in the latter years was called into conference with the Board, and the general plan of campaign agreed upon. But thereafter they were allowed to work unhampered by pre-censorship. It is hard for any one to write spontaneously with a consciousness of criticism always impending. Therefore, save in instances where some particular accuracy was essential we have never tried to O. K. press material before it was sent out, but merely to discuss and criticize, if necessary, after publication. The chance error is, I believe, much less important than the curtailing of the sense of personal responsibility and spontaneous impulse on the part of the writer. And I am sure that no one could have injected into the department the alert and dynamic atmosphere which it seems to me to have, had he been constantly conscious of critical worry on the part of the executive or the other members of the Board.

The function of play reading which is, in a way, the heart-beat of any producing organization, has had to be assigned with the greatest care. We were fortunate to find, after the death of Josephine Meyer, some one who so ably understood the requirements of Guild standards as Courtenay Lemon. His wide reading and knowledge, not only of the theatre, past and present, but of allied cultural subjects, and the militant liberalism of his mental attitude made his judgment approximate with sympathy and reliability that of the members of the Board. As the manuscripts became more numerous, Anita Block was added to take care of foreign plays and Harold Clurman came into Mr. Lemon's department. The Board can never, of course, be sure of agreeing with its play readers, and personal prejudices on both sides must be discounted, but without an underlying similarity of feeling about the fundamentals of life and literature, no play reports could be of real value to us. This is why the choice of play readers must always be a difficult and important one for organizations such as ours.

The most difficult department of all to build up satisfactorily has been that of production. After Augustin Duncan's resignation from the Board, we turned to Emanuel Reicher. At that time, Philip Moeller was too much a part of our own group to be seen at his true value. We were afraid to hitch our wagon to his inexperienced star. And it took us some years to realize that Moeller was developing as producer with the same strides that the Guild was developing as an organization. Subsequently, he became a pillar of strength in the production department. And Dudley Digges could also be counted upon to take over a certain burden of production. Various other directors were tried for occasional plays, and from each of them we learned excellent lessons — lessons varying from the skilled professionalism of Robert Milton and the direct competence of Frank Reicher to the theatrically naïve, but artistically interesting, efforts of Stark Young and the plastic effectiveness of Lee Simonson, both of whom made their first and perhaps only productions for the Guild. For one season we brought Komisarshevsky over from London, and a very stimulating experience it was for us all. But as the Guild grew, we were conscious of the increasing need for another permanent director to attach to the organization,

The Theatre Guild

and the final recognition of Rouben Mamoulian, after he had served a year's apprenticeship in the Guild School, and our welcoming him into our ranks with his startling and beautiful staging of "Porgy," was an important event in the production history of the Guild.

But the problem of developing new material is always a difficult one because, lacking the opportunity of try-outs, the responsibility for a New York production of Guild calibre is a heavy one to impose on inexperienced talent and demands on the part of the Guild Board a willingness to take almost unjustifiable risks. The theory that inexperienced material can be tried out in the position of assistant director is, to my mind, essentially false. For there is no position as anomalous as that of an assistant director — except in productions so large that component parts may be treated as separate units. But in our theatre, the gesture of production is sufficiently broken or limited by the criticism of the Board of Managers, and an assistant director who tries to do more than be an excellent stage manager, carrying out the ideas of his chief, would only be a source of irritation and interruption to the director himself. The more creative the assistant is, therefore, the more probably will he be at variance with the gesture of the man to whom he must be subordinate. For that reason we have given up the use of assistant directors, trying to give prospective directing material the chance for experience, if not opportunity, in the position of stage manager.

It is perhaps because the critical and constructive function of the Board itself, in connection with production, has been such an integral part of our organization that it has been found the most difficult to substitute for or delegate in any way. But it is now our hope to be able to revive in somewhat altered form the special productions of our earlier years, which will give creative opportunity to the younger members of the organization to try their hands not only at production, but at helping to choose, helping to prepare, helping to criticize, and helping to act in plays of experimental quality. I hope that by the time this book appears, such an experimental department will be not only planned but an actuality. It presents many difficulties but it gives us also something more to think and worry about — without which the game of the theatre would cease to interest us.

THE GUILD AND PRODUCTION

By Philip Moeller

Of all forms of human expression, complicated and simple, none, I think, when the final result is achieved, is taken so immediately for granted as the theatre. I hesitate to use the phrase "art of the theatre," because I know only too well how often an empty inadequacy can hide behind an elaborate terminology. And when, instead, I say "work in the theatre," it doesn't mean that I do not thoroughly realize that any important aesthetic expression that truly justifies itself must be, in its essential essence, an art.

Audiences, for the most part, accept the solution of the producer's problems as if all of them had inevitably to be worked out that way. And they do this naturally enough, because an average audience, unless some of this audience has been in on the game — and from a perfectly valid point of view the theatre might be defined as a game of interpreting life played in public — has absolutely no realization of the tremendous net of interplaying complexities which have to be adjusted and solved before the finished living message of the produced play is presented to them. There are probably in the far too many books about the "art of the theatre" very fulsome explanations and rules for the seemingly easy and final solution of most of these problems, but I am afraid I have not too great a sympathy with the school or academic approach to the theatre. I do not think that a real result in the theatre is ever the result of any amount of theorizing, no matter how high-sounding or deep-meaning it may seem. I have reiterated — possibly on too many occasions — both in print and out of it, that nothing is more futile than "talk" about the theatre, even when the talk is seemingly profoundly written and charmingly illustrated with all sorts of arty photographs and complicated, measured diagrams and full of what seem to be easy helps on the hard, high road of the journey. Indeed, one might as well "talk" a beautiful woman or a Beethoven symphony. The theatre, in its truest essence (and, of course, here I omit the history of dramatic literature and studies of what I think is called "dramaturgy" for the lack of a better name), is a living thing, living at a particular time and dying or going to glory because of the living reaction of a living audience. Not all the elocution of a dramatically disposed Demosthenes or the theories of an art theatre Aristotle ever put a play over. If the play "gets over," as we say in the theatre — and if the phrase is analyzed, it will be seen that it is a most explicit one — if the play gets over, as I say, it is because it contains the combination of elements that inevitably make the audience want to accept it. In fact, I think this idea could be evolved, if thoroughly thought out, to make a pretty good case for the statement, which on the surface may seem very fantastic, that in a certain very real reality it is the audience that gives the performance of a play; the actors and the playwright and the director, in a deftly subtle way — and to a large extent totally unconscious to themselves — have simply created an accumulation of interacting psychological stimuli, which result in a certain reaction on the part of the audience.

And this is one of the reasons why the phrase, "Nothing succeeds like success," is so happily applicable to the theatre; because the bigger the house, the more numerous are these possible instruments of reaction to stimuli. In the last analysis — and this in spite of the enthusiastic specialist — the truth of the theatre must be a general truth; and among the thousands there are more apt to be sensitive instruments of reaction to the excitement of truth than among the few. I am perpetually feeling the theatre in the terms of this sort of popular communication. I use the word "popular" rather with its connotation in the direction of population than in trying to imply an interpretation which obviously I do not mean — namely, that all art must necessarily be "popular" or easy, in the accepted sense of the word. But the greater we can make the general appeal of a play, even if its theme is special — and many of the Guild plays have had such themes — the greater chance it has for a greater audience to give a fine " show " of its reactions. Because of this spontaneous, mutual, life-giving reaction between the actors and an audience, each new show in which the actors are worthy of the name is really a new creation, and in the long run I think people who care for the theatre and will go on caring for it in the face of attacks from all sides will realize that this quality of new creation will be one of the final victorious answers to that noisy army of blaring banners, the talkies, which at the moment and possibly a little too hopefully premature are so raucously and incessantly blowing their brassy trumpets to celebrate what they so enthusiastically know will be our long deserved eventual and unavoidable annihilation in the competitive battle of this art or business of giving plays.

We of the Guild are being perpetually bombarded with questions, oral and written, as to why we have done or are doing a certain sort of play. I have often tried to arrive at some sort of conclusive answer. The nearest I can get to it is the realization that any script that we select for production has to contain at its best the combination of two essentials. These essentials are: the quality of its theme and the quality of its treatment. Often an idea of extraordinary possibilities goes to its death because of an inadequacy of treatment; and also often an idea of no original tremendous importance can be lifted into something of fascinating quality by the manner of its treatment. But, of course, the great play is an inevitable combination of both these

The Theatre Guild

elements. The Guild, as our history shows, has never been omniscient in its choice of plays. We have made many mistakes, against which with all due modesty I am proud to list our few victories. But in no instance, whether the play were a success or a failure, have we selected it for the more obvious reasons of its commercial possibilities. The six of us have always felt, rightly or wrongly, and as the result of an eventual majority vote or as near as we could get to it, that the play we were going to do had either of these two elements, either an importance of theme or an importance of treatment, and, in the happiest conclusions, both of these.

I have mentioned the six of us, and I wish from the beginning to emphasize that, because, when all is said and done, this group expression is the most original and, judging from results, the most constructive contribution to the history of the theatre, or at least to the history of the art of the theatre in America, that the Guild has made. A Guild production is, to a very large extent, the expression of a group directorate, and when I say directorate I use the word least in the executive sense. I mean that, as almost unbelievable as it sounds, a Guild production is the result of the reaction of six — and sometimes seven — people, utilizing a person most practically and sensitively equipped to project and realize the ideas of us all. Now, to the average director, and to a person but casually acquainted with the work of production, this assuredly sounds from the start as a thing so exaggeratedly impossible that somehow it couldn't work. The answer to this is that it has worked, and I am sure that many of our distinguished guest stage directors will acknowledge what I so definitely feel — that the reaction of the group of directors has been, to a large extent, the explanation of much that has distinguished and enriched what is known as " a Guild production." There have been six or seven minds at work on the problem. There have been six and at times seven minds, each different and varied in response, reacting to the stimuli the director has created before the result is presented to the public. In certain instances, a more sensitively acute reaction has shown the way for an emphasis in some particular direction, and this has also worked conversely; because, where the director has felt that his idea has carried, often to the point of an excruciating obviousness, he has found that what has seemed to him as direct as a shot in the very centre of the bull's-eye has gone over the heads and hearts of his auditors — and then one of the six, or two of the six — choose the number as you will, speak up and say, " What does that mean, if you have meant it to mean anything at all? " And then the embarrassed director, if he is an artist — and in the last analysis, he must be an artist in humility — realizes that the secret which he thinks he has told is still a secret and it is then he begins to communicate, if he knows his job, in a language of clearer and more tangible generalities.

Now, when I say that a Guild production is the expression of a group, I do not for an instant wish to imply that the director's stamp is not inevitably on his job. The committee sit in as a body of critics, rather than creators; but often — much more often in fact than the public realizes — their criticism is in the nature of creation. A director rightly equipped has to be a person of very subtle sensitivity and also a technician who can sense when an idea is constructive and who comes to know, sooner or later, where the lack of immediate response must point to a weakness in the scheme of his projection.

Very often the Guild has realized that the theme of a play was so difficult that the audience would be forced to an unusual effort to get its message. In every instance of this sort, this has intensified our effort, as far as we knew how, to achieve an intenser clarification of interpretation. Often indeed, in such plays for instance as Werfel's "Goat Song," the theme has perhaps been so fraught with complexities that we weren't always absolutely sure ourselves of the final direction of certain scenes in the script. In instances like that, and when they come along they are rare and of a stimulating excitement, someone speaks up out of the exuberance of enthusiastic clairvoyance and seems to tell the rest of us. Somehow we were all trying for the truth, and Ben Ami, who so beautifully realized the possibilities of "Goat Song," was in spirit and in fact along with us; and out of all this enthusiastic questioning came at least an answer which we felt, within the limits of our limitations, pointed at least in the true direction of Werfel's intention in his extraordinary play.

We have learned our method step by step by the production of some seventy plays, including one or two revivals of certain of our successes and by a most careful reproduction of our shows for the road; and when I read over the list of our varied performances, I react with a certain pride which I am sure is felt by all of us to the range and variety of the work we have done.

Let me enumerate briefly what I think are some of the finer contributions that our guest directors have made for us. Those who remember it have nothing but enthusiasm for the fine, direct simplicity with which Augustin Duncan handled our first, and possibly our most important, success — because it enabled us to go on — St. John Ervine's "John Ferguson" of our first season. And then following was the superb work of Emanuel Reicher on Tolstoi's "Power of Darkness" and on "Jane Clegg." Personally, I look back on "father Reicher" as the most inspirational person that it has ever been the good fortune of the Guild directors to have associated with them. He was, to me, the finest artist in the theatre that I have ever known. He was that rare and extraordinary combination — a superb technician and, in the finest sense, a mystic at the same time. I shall never forget one day when I was baffled by some tremendous complexity in a production. I remember that dear old Reicher came upon me in my despair and I didn't have to tell him what was the matter. A poet — and after all a poet is the practical mystic who knows how, I think — doesn't have to be told. He said to me: "Do what I do. Don't bother about it. Just sit back and wait, and it will come to you." And indeed it did; and I have never forgotten this. In fact, I think I could resolve it into a sort of an aesthetic theory, if it weren't that I have an innate terror of the possibility of a theory being a finality — and this because I know that any final finality is death, both in life and in art. But at least what he said to me contained the germ of a thought. An artist is one who through years of arduous technical work has prepared himself for the moment when the urge of creation comes to him — for that thrilling moment when the worker becomes the instrument for that surge of inspiration which finds its richest response in the communication of what is most moving, either to laughter or tears, in the hearts of humanity.

Then, as I glance down the list of our plays, I am appalled at, and at the same time proud of, our divine temerity in attempting Shaw's colossal trilogy of " Back to Methuselah." This play which took three nights to do and which a patient, and I fear in the case of " Methuselah " a tolerant posterity alone will properly evaluate in some eventual consideration of Shaw's undeniable greatness, was for a certainty a sign of our extraordinary courage and our dogged determination to experiment. We had made some surplus money the season before and so we felt that we could afford to lose some in a worthy, though lengthy, cause. And so, toward the end of our fourth season (1921–22), we began rehearsals of the colossus with a splendid youthful enthusiasm and an equally young disregard of the staggering difficulties of the trilogy. On the whole, I think we came off pretty well. I still wonder how the actors ever learnt the parts, though this wonder is slightly tempered since "Strange Interlude," and how we ever managed to knit together the tremendously involved complexities of the trilogy as a whole. It was my job to be general director of the progress of this more or less dramatic philosophical elephant of a play, and I remember most happily the splendid work of Alice Lewisohn and Agnes Morgan in the first part, and again, the fine assistance of Frank Reicher throughout the rest.

The production of "Back to Methuselah" was the occasion of one of Shaw's characteristic remarks which, I think, is worthy of record. We had planned, if I remember rightly, to lose at the time a total of about $30,000. And when our final loss summed up to something about twenty, and Shaw heard of this, he remarked in his inimitable manner, "That is how I save the Guild money." But it was William, our loyal doorman, who has been so courteously receiving our carriage customers from the very beginning some ten years ago at the Garrick Theatre, who has stamped "Methuselah" in my mind with its brightest anecdote. One night Wertheim, I think, asked him how the show was going. "Boss," he answered, "better and better every evening; less people are leaving before it is over." Several years later I told this to Shaw, who is probably the wittiest man in Europe, but somehow — as we say in our picturesque vernacular, "he didn't seem to get it." Or maybe he did.

Our list of plays is, I think, a pretty long one, even for ten years of work, and when I read it over, I recall particularly

The Theatre Guild

Dudley Digges' splendid handling of the several Shaw scripts that he has done for us; the fine sense of the theatre that Robert Milton showed in " He Who Gets Slapped "; the younger Reicher's superb realization of Molnar's none-too-easy " Liliom "; and how beautifully and sensitively Stark Young projected the subtlest overtones of the Lenormand play, " The Failures." It was this production, too, which gave Simonson his chance to experiment with a new technique of scenery, called for in the innumerable swift shifts of the script. The actors and Young and Simonson achieved a rare beauty in " The Failures." I don't think any of us or our audience will ever forget the clear and luminous beauty of the production.

Then came Komisarshevsky, who, at the suggestion of Langner, left London to come to New York and direct for us. I think, in many ways, he was one of the most interesting and original of our guest producers. His production of " The Tidings Brought to Mary," while unsuccessful from the point of view of a box-office public, was a thing of extraordinary beauty to the few who got it. It was Komisarshevsky's very original experiment in a plastic or sculptural method of production. If the play failed, it was possibly because our audiences were not as yet ready for it, or because Komisarshevsky's method, combined with the extreme difficulty of the theme of Claudel's play, resulted in a too esoteric and baffling sort of mystification; or perhaps because it was the Guild's furthest excursion, up to that time, into the remote realms of the special. He was more successful, from the public's point of view, in his superb " Peer Gynt " of our fifth season. And in the following year, Lee Simonson, our scenic director, took his first — and I hope not his last — whack at production. He achieved certain superb pictorial moments of arrested crowd action in " Man and the Masses," a play which, from the beginning, I personally felt was too specifically Germanic and parochial in its appeal for an American audience. But I am glad he lived through the job. In his secret mind I think he bravely treasures some of the scars of the conflict to this day. Always a keen critic, he came out more expertly equipped in the direction of constructive help. The next season's end saw " The Garrick Gaieties "; and while this delicious show had very little to do with production *per se,* I cannot read over the catalogue of our accomplishments without stopping for a moment to acknowledge my deep debt of gratitude to " the kids " — some since come into fame — who put this over. There wasn't much production in the show, but there was a spirit of gaiety and delicious *élan vital* of life which was like a forbidden liqueur at the end of the six years' hor d'oeuvres of hope and the actual meal of realization. The Gaieties show is one of my happiest remembrances of the Guild and its past.

Our eighth season saw Ben Ami's stupendous job and fine result on Werfel's " Goat Song." The next year saw John Cromwell's fine shading of " The Silver Cord," Copeau's famous production of " Karamazov," which I cannot mention without recalling the splendid spirit of coöperation and vital personal stimulus that the great French director was for all of us. It was a splendid privilege to have him with us, and some day I hope he will be coming back to do another play for the Guild, because he too is what the elder Reicher was — that extraordinary combination, an artist who after long and arduous years of living practice in the living theatre is still aflame with a youthful ageless exuberance of inspiration. The ninth season also saw my own job in " Right You Are If You Think You Are," which in many ways, with the possible exception of Lawson's fine " Processional " and O'Neill's epical history of *Nina Leeds*, was perhaps the most fascinating of all the thirty-four theatre problems which I have tried to help solve for the Guild. Now we have come to our tenth season which brought a new and important figure into the little world of worthwhile directors in the American theatre. It opened with Rouben Mamoulian's deservedly famous production of " Porgy," one of the Guild's most splendid successes and, I think, one of the most original, colorful, and finest productions ever done in the American theatre. The same season again saw Digges' work in " The Doctor's Dilemma," and at the season's end my own production of " Strange Interlude," of which I think enough has been said for me to spare the reader any further accounting here.

The phrase, " A Guild Production," has become a sort of sign-post of quality in the American theatre. Obviously, with pride tempered by humility, we are all of us proud of what it stands for. And when I say " all of us," I should like to mention, if only too briefly, how often I have had the most helpful suggestions from my actors — ideas which over and over again have been of valuable aid in the process of rehearsals. And then, too, there are many others who have received less public recognition than some of us, but who were and are still most valuable props to the Theatre Guild staff.

Some fifteen years of experiment in theatre production have taught me what I suppose any sensible scholar learns along the way of the difficult journey, and that is that my work as director — in fact, the work of the Guild as a producing organization — is, in a sense, always just beginning. Possibly, in my own case, the germ of it began centuries ago in the secret thoughts of my forebears; that is for the psychologist and the scientist in evolution to answer, if it is worth the trouble. Possibly it was finding itself in the basement prestidigitator performances that I used to inflict on an all too patient and kindly family, and possibly, it was risking its life when as a kid and when I ought to have been in bed, on late Spring evenings, I used to sneak downstairs and lean over the backyard balcony of my grandfather's house to watch the scarlet feet of the chorus ladies weaving their visual, soul-ensnaring counterpoint, which I could just glimpse through the fire-escape which the beginning heat and the good gods of my future had opened, when that infamous shrine of Victorian vice, Koster and Bials, was holding its wickedly innocent orgies in the old days on 34th Street.

The Theatre Guild

It might be interesting, at least to myself, to attempt some sort of psychological analysis as to why I am a director; but this is hardly the place for it. This is a chapter of Guild history, and not my own. As I have said, I function as a member of a group; and while I can only reiterate my sense of indebtedness for their constructive criticism and help, there is still a larger group which all of us realize has been so vast a part of the history of the Guild — and this is our audience. If the Guild has grown, it is because our audience has grown. There is very definitely a Theatre Guild audience, as well as a Theatre Guild production. If we approach the interpretation of each new script with an ever alive enthusiasm and what we all hope is an ever-growing proficiency in practice, it is because our system of subscribers assures us, during the first critical weeks of a production, an audience of intelligent friends alive to our success, critical of our failures, but always keenly interested in our development. As I have said, the living theatre, in its final analysis, is a place of living communication — the more varied and democratic, the nearer to the ideas and ideals of the Guild.

And as for myself, I do not — and never will — believe in the anarchistic idea in any of the arts, and least of all in the art of theatric production. I believe that an audience comes to the theatre, and rightly and justly so, to find out. And I believe that no director is worthy of the name who holds to the theory that his particular contribution is of such isolated quality that no one can ever understand it but himself. If his ideas are of such unique importance as to be worth anything, and utterly original at the same time (and I doubt if this has ever really happened in any branch of aesthetic expression), it is precisely then that the work of the director in the theatre most truly begins. He must interpret his ideas for others. He must, so to speak, tell his secret in terms of a message that can be understood. Otherwise, let him sit alone with his precious theories in his ivory tower on the lonely island of smug superiority, and not come down into the market place of the world, and not attempt to preach in that most popular temple of the people, which in its finest sense the theatre was, and is, and will be.

AN ART THEATRE WITHOUT ENDOWMENT

By *Maurice Wertheim*

One day in the early years of the Theatre Guild, I think it was in talking to John Corbin at our third birthday dinner in 1922, I found myself first voicing to one outside our group an idea I had held for a long time. It was the thought that an art theatre, contrary to established precedent, would be more solidly built without an endowment than with one. While this conception had guided us from the beginning we had, up to that time, done so little to prove it valid and the world was so skeptical of such a possibility, that there had been little use of trying to argue it with others. In looking back I can now see that that talk with Corbin marked a significant moment, since evidently things had begun so to shape themselves with the Guild that it seemed justifiable to assert as a principle that which theretofore had been a tentative hope. Corbin, even with his broad sympathy for everything new in the theatre, could not quite swallow it and cleverly remarked that we six directors were really endowing the Guild by serving at little or no salary when the same services might well have commanded a considerable price in the commercial theatre. It is true that he had me there; but if that be endowment it is the only one the Guild ever received and it is the only one I hope it ever will have.

This matter of an endowment and the stress laid on whether you have one or not may seem strange to some. But to me it is at the foundation of the entire structure; it shapes its character and determines its future, chiefly for the reason that I cannot see how a theatre can either be permanent or truly vital and in touch with its time unless it is self-supporting.

The question of permanence seems obvious. The usual practice of starting art theatres in this country is to surround the enterprise with a number of decorative committees, carefully chosen with an eye to financial or social backing, and enlist their numbers each year in a private or public campaign to make up the deficit. The deficit! What an ogre — what a terrible sword of Damocles always overhanging the work of artists truly in touch with their time! Overpowered by the so-called practical men in their field, they come to feel that, commercially speaking, only the most commonplace things can possibly have a chance of paying their way. Therefore, it has become almost a superstition to rely on the generosity of princes, without realizing at the start that by that very action the permanence of the enterprise is doomed. For, while there are new princes to take the place of those who fall away, yet the time is bound to come at moments of failure or unpopularity or bad times or whatnot, that this road will prove a blind alley and the enterprise be crushed under the landslide of the deficit.

And of course when you expect a deficit you usually have one, whether you need to or not. That is one of the strangest things about artists. They simply cannot conceive that the practical men in their field may be wrong and that they — the artists — may possess within themselves something which, when combined with careful management and unremitting attention to business detail, can far outstrip the work of those who look upon the proposition as a matter of pure gain. If there is one message I should like to send to those younger people who are considering the starting of art theatre enterprises it is this: Do not be disturbed by movies, squawkies, or the commercial theatre, even if you have little money. The public wants the best — not the worst — and if you have it in you to provide them with the best and are willing to work hard, you can become self-supporting as well as successful.

However, beyond the question of permanence lies the question of vitality. When I say " vitality," I do not refer to the question of artistic control or muzzling which so often accompanies financial dependence. That, of course, is primary, and any idea that independence of action can go side by side with dependence on money is a comfortable rationalization with which many ambitious directors have deluded themselves since the year 1 of the art theatre. What I do refer to and what I consider even more important is the relation with one's public — that indefinable "feel" as to what is in the air, as to what belongs to your time, not esoteric, not recondite and not artificial. By that I do not mean that an art theatre should not attempt to lead its public; it should. But in order to know what the great public is really thinking about and what ideas are vital to them — not merely to you — then I feel you must always be selling tickets to them; experience the deep pleasure of creating something that holds them, as well as the deep despair of empty houses.

I do not deny that there is a place for the purely experimental theatre which, supported by the generosity of a few patrons, keeps on producing plays which in the judgment of their directors are worth while, irrespective of whether the public comes or not. There is no question but that out of such movements progress is at all times made in the theatre, and new dramatists and actors discovered. To my mind, however, the field of such an enterprise is special and its influence limited. It is by no means less worthy than the type of institution the Guild has tried to build; it is merely different.

Furthermore, I feel that in an institution which supports itself and is in the closest touch with the taste of the public by being dependent on it, the possibility always lies of being experimental to a salutary degree. It is obvious that if you are seeking to influence the dramatic life of your community in a larger way, you will not be able to do it by being experimental all the time. We of the Guild have always made it a rule never to let a season pass without some production, and often more than one, of an experimental nature, and always delighted in the commercial success of an average play to have the funds to produce some work of new departure. Witness, for example, "Back to Methuselah," "Processional," "Goat Song," and even "Strange Interlude."

Some of our detractors will probably laugh in their sleeves at this attitude toward profit on the part of the Guild — particularly now that we are large and every now and then financially successful to a very unexpected degree. "The idea," they would say, "that the Guild delights in profitable productions merely to put on experimental ones!" We have been called canny producers by some, shrewd business men by others, and have even been accused of being bunk-artists who, under cover of an artistic goal, rake in the public's shekels for personal profit. I admit that it is difficult for any one to understand the attitude of six young people starting ten years ago with a passionate desire to be free and untrammelled in their expression, determined to build something that would be permanent, and convinced that they would only be completely in touch with their time if they were self-supporting. To do this, our whole thought from the beginning was, "We must keep our heads above water," financially speaking. Everything except artistic integrity had to be sacrificed to that, for if artistic integrity were lost, there would be no use in doing the thing at all. We happened to be six people who loved the theatre more than we loved commercial rewards and we did not care a great deal as long as we were putting on the plays we wanted to do and at the same time were working toward permanently averting bankruptcy. That is the explanation of the extreme parsimony in the matter of actors' salaries for which we had the reputation in our early years; but the unremitting work and meticulous attention to every detail which it took to avoid bankruptcy also explains part of our present success. Naturally with such evidence of careful business management before them, it is difficult for our commercial competitors to understand how the enterprise can be other than a commercial one. But that simply neglects the factor that we were determined to avoid the pitfalls into which we had seen similar enterprises fall in the past. At no time that I can remember was a play ever produced or left unproduced because of its box office draw; in fact we became superstitious, through much experience, that the plays that were thought to have no box office draw usually possessed it. In other words, we are, after ten years of work, convinced that the more fully you adhere to your ideal, the more thoroughly will the public support you.

Of course, in addition to the most careful economy, personal sacrifices by each member of the group have been at all times necessary, and not only in the matter of money. It may be interesting to the public to know that even today each member of the Board draws a salary of $25 per week in addition to percentages of receipts above expenses, now quite lucrative; but the $25 weekly is the survival of the custom established the first week, and for a number of years it was practically all that was received. In fact, on several occasions of financial distress, I recall that all directors waived their salaries until better times should appear. One of these occasions was after the production of Tolstoi's "Power of Darkness," which, while an artistic success, reduced our funds in bank to $100 with bills of $200 to meet. We all met in emergency meeting in the small library in the basement of the Garrick Theatre, hoping that by some bolt from the blue a good play, possible of economical production, would occur to us, since in those days we had no funds to have plays on hand. Old Emanuel Reicher, who had produced for us, attended the meeting and we all discussed and suggested plays for hours. The bolt from the blue fell, but in a peculiar way. Reicher, who was sitting with chair tipped back between me and the bookshelves, suddenly tipped back a bit too far and steadied himself by putting one hand on the shelves. His fingers caught on a book which after awhile he pulled out and which I saw him examine with growing interest. Suddenly he said, "Why don't you do this play? It is by the man who wrote one of your first successes." That play was "Jane Clegg" by St. John Ervine, author of "John Ferguson." We put it on for practically nothing, and it ran for many months, actually saving the Guild and restoring the $25 weekly to the directors.

The First Ten Years

But the matter of financial sacrifice was as nothing compared with the sacrifice of individual expression on the part of the directors. Every member of the group had his or her particular talent in the theatre and many times the temptation to make the Guild the vehicle of that talent was almost too strong to resist. This is probably the rock on which most group expressions break. But slowly and surely it was borne in on us that the Guild was bigger than any one of us and it became entirely evident that the only chance we had of success was to submerge our own individualities and make the thing a collective expression. That was probably the most difficult hurdle we had to clear, but also probably the most essential.

All of this may sound as if we believe that our success in creating an art theatre without endowment was due entirely to sacrifices and work on our part. The contrary is the case, for we know full well that without the support and encouragement of an intelligent theatre-going public all our work would have been for nothing. The subscription system we use is a good illustration of this. We started it the first year, offering to subscribers a season's attendance at each one of our six plays at somewhat reduced prices, together with lecture and other privileges. The idea has proved to be a sound one because with enough subscriptions to cover cost of production, one's possible loss is greatly minimized. I need not relate here how our subscription list grew from 150 the first year to over 60,000 during the current year, about evenly divided between New York on the one hand and our road cities on the other; but the point is that while we may have devised the system the public responded. This is not due only to the fact that the majority of our plays may have appealed to them with growing force and that we happened on the theatrical horizon at a propitious time. I firmly believe that a much larger section of the public than is generally conceived are constantly seeking the best in the theatre, and when they see a group who are making an honest effort to give them something beyond that which they are supposed to want, they come forward generously whether they approve of all plays or not. It is this spirit on the part of the American public — more idealistic in my opinion than any other — which has really been our endowment.

THE ACTOR'S RELATION TO THE ART THEATRE AND VICE VERSA

By Helen Westley

In speaking of the relation of the actor to the art theatre, it is necessary to point out that there is no " collective " point of view toward an emotion. A relation to any art must be a personal relation, or it is not a relation at all but a tradition. Therefore, it is in terms of myself that I speak of things that are not myself. What I was ten years ago, what I am today, what I once visioned and what I now see — that is my approach.

It goes back even further than this. What I felt toward the Guild ten years ago was most superbly based upon my youthful emotional life; and that in turn was firmly embedded in idealism. " Ideals " is just another term for " twenty." Youth is idealistic, idiotic and splendid in that it is in these years that one is spendthrift with an account that can after all be spent only when it is " too late." The coin that personal youth strives gallantly to squander can be drawn upon only in impersonal years — in those years, in other words, when the eye is not filled with *the* person, but by persons. Youth has relations with the world; age has relations toward the world.

Ten years ago I was still subjective. Now I know that what I hoped to spend on life can be spent only in the theatre. My personal ambition has gone into the objective art of the drama. So it becomes clear that my relation to the theatre ten years ago was not what it is today.

Today, having been cast, against my will, for endless hags and harridans — this insidious plot against me having been hatched the moment I accepted the part of the old lady who helped kill the baby in " The Power of Darkness " — I no longer lament my lot. I croak and croon and screech with the *élan* of Socrates turning his argument against himself. I paint a hundred years upon my face with the sole wish that I may live to be two hundred, when it will become necessary for Shaw to write a part for a woman of a thousand that I may overstep my years with my accustomed traditional calm. The art theatre has seen me through my hours of idealism, when I wanted to be high-handed and witty and handsome; relentlessly, wig upon wig, crutch upon crutch, groan upon groan, they have led me into the philosophic cabbage patch of Voltairean laughter, where, to paraphrase, no one is thwarted and no one grows young. Ten years ago I was eager — I may have even been ambitious, though that has not been strong in the Meseroles since the Huguenots stood for the faith —

and ended as that "character Helen." Then I was glad to draw $25 on my part in the world. Now I am glad to draw many times that for my part in the Guild. Today I am midwife to any baby. If when I smack it, it weeps, so much the better. If I smack and there is no response — well, I have yet to behold that baby! I am not fool enough to want to play *Juliet* even if the Guild would let me, and the only taint of that earlier ambition is a wonderment as to where the good parts for the woman over forty have hidden themselves.

Let us turn the baby over. What is the art theatre's relation to the actor and to the audience? The art theatre differs from the popular theatre in that it presents, or strives to present, dramas by artists who have their imagination so wedded to the medium necessary to its best portrayal that the one — purely technical — makes of the other — purely emotional — a perfect whole.

This nicety, in turn, affects the actors. The popular play presents the actor; the actor of the art theatre presents a play. It is self-evident that the art theatre is not a hunting ground for authors who write for the sole purpose of making money. It is also as obvious that the art theatre is not the haven of the "star." This, in its turn, affects the public. The public patronizes both theatres, it is true — but not for the same reasons.

The popular theatre is sustained by mass worship of a certain actor or actress. This public does not swarm to see So-and-So's play. They swarm to see So-and-So act. This audience is in what might be called the "family state of mind." The actor here is "one of them." They have seen him or her play since they can remember. They know what their idol eats, reads, thinks, what she wears, and whom she has married. Will she be the same this season? Will she still smile with the crooked smile, lisp with the delightful lisp of yesteryear, in that play by What's-his-name? They are interested primarily in the arc of that person — the cradle-to-the-grave gesture.

The audience of the art theatre is interested in the other side of the story, or largely so. They are curious about the mind of man, and what this ego can, through its actors, teach them to expect of people and of life.

Will this year's Eugene O'Neill or last year's Shaw make Miss X or Mr. Z a little more truly Shaw, a little more exactly O'Neill? They are there to see what art can do with its people, the actors, and what art's citizens can do with their public, the audience.

Therefore, the actor's relation to the art theatre is one of respect and service. This tends to dim the ego. In adhering truthfully to a great script there is something of religion. The play is the star.

The art theatre actor learns, sooner or later, that he is not a separate entity, though he must be a personal entity. He knows that he must make himself a part of the whole. Every unit is as important as every other unit. "There are no little parts," said Stanislavsky; "there are only little actors."

The First Ten Years

The producer knows that to round out a play each actor must be a perfectly fitting section of the original design, and when this is accomplished, the audience has almost sat with Hamlet at the hour when Shakespeare created him.

The art theatre is a sort of glorified Poor House. It harbors all states of mind and all kinds of matter; Poor House in that no one may enter who cannot count his scars with a ferocious immunity; no one who has not gone past a personal relation to himself; not the beaten person, but the person who has conquered personal identification. Ego, in its pure form, is consciousness of the cause of which it is the effect — as the lava is the consciousness of the volcano. The only actor who is even wiser than this is he who is in a continual condition of cause — the volcano that burns and does not destroy. Such a person is rarely found upon any stage, because such a person is rarely found in life. He is seldom born, and when he is he is usually banked up in the drama of existence, where he is at his worst.

How many people will step aside for the greater integrity of a situation? There have been a few, but you could count upon the fingers of your hand the actors who have stepped aside for the greater integrity of the part — and should one such be found, it will be in the art theatre; and even so, I predict that you will look under many a rug, tear up many a mattress and toss tear-bombs into many a wing and dressing-room before you bag one.

You may find him in my Voltairean cabbage patch, combing out my ninetieth wig — and you may not!

SETTING THE STAGE

By Lee Simonson

I

A TELEPHONE call from Philip Moeller prompted me to become a scenic designer; a letter from Lawrence Langner made the theatre my profession. Langner's appeal reached me soon after the Armistice at Camp Sherman while I was still in a "shavetail's" uniform waiting to be demobilized: the spirit and the purpose of the old Washington Square Players had not died; would I help to revive it in a new organization? I shared his conviction and, a few months later at his apartment in New York, became one of the Guild's directors and spent our first meetings trying to convince him that without an endowment no art theatre could survive! Moeller's 'phone five years previous was more casual: they needed a set at the Band Box for the new bill. Wouldn't I like to try one? I did and entered the world of back stage for the first time.

The First Ten Years

Trained as a painter, decorative design had always held the center of my interest, but I had never remotely associated it with the stage, although I had cheered Isadora Duncan's debut in Paris, fought for balcony seats for every Russian ballet season at the Châtelet, witnessed the riot at the first performance of "l'Après-midi d'un Faune," collected souvenir programs with colored reproductions of Bakst's decors and his costumes and stowed them away in my portfolios. During two summers at Munich I followed Rhinehardt's repertoire at the Künstler Theatre, including *Sumurun* and the then unknown Moissi as *Hamlet* in Fritz Erler's settings, and absorbed the theory of the decorative *Relief Bühne*. Later at Lugné Poë's *Théâtre de l'Oeuvre*, I saw the Karlsruh Theatre give Andreiev's "Life of Man," then a highly exotic and mystifying script, in a stylized production that anticipated most of the expressionism and constructivism of ten years later.

Probably I had always been more interested in the theatre than I realized. As a Harvard undergraduate in the remote days of 1905 to 1908, I had preached Shaw as "greater than Molière" to unbelievers and in English 47 failed to convince Professor Baker that G. B. S. was worth more than a single lecture. Walter Lippmann used to wave his hand at my bookcase and remark, "Authority on literature since 1900." The first published volumes of Synge's plays were part of the collection. With certain literati among the upper-classmen who occasionally encouraged me to visit them, I read Yeats aloud, argued the world significance of the Abbey Theatre and the Celtic revival, and very nearly gave Charles Townsend Copeland cardiac convulsions with my purple and mauve prose in attempting to imitate the "Land of Heart's Desire." I can remember how upset some of us were at having missed a visiting Irishwoman who gave a recital in some Cambridge church, reading Yeats to the accompaniment of a psaltery. I concluded my academic efforts with a lengthy thesis, violently attacking the Poetics for not having anticipated Ibsen.

Not unfamiliar then with the drama's Bible and a good many of its most modern experiments I walked on to the diminutive stage of the Band Box and found that the problem (as I have found it ever since) was a pragmatic one and not a matter of dogma, of theory or preconception as to what the art of the theatre should or should not be. I faced the necessity, as a craftsman, of meeting a concrete predicament with as much imagination as possible. As an avowed pragmatist my first problem did not "phase" me.

The play was Andreiev's "Love of One's Neighbor"; the situation, the usual motley of tourists on a mountain top agog and aghast at the sight of a mountain climber about to fall off a neighboring cliff. He proves to be tied there by the proprietor of the nearby *bierstube* as a bait to attract more visitors and to delay their departure until, due to the excitement, they had consumed more than their usual number of *schoppen*.

How was a flat stage to be transformed into a mountain

top? It could not be cut with traps, no one could climb up out of the cellar; no seemingly solid cliff could be built; the budget would not allow it even if there had been room. In fact I was shown one canvas flat abandoned by the previous tenant and told I might paint it any color and nick it into any shape, but that was all the scenery I could have.

I finally suggested hoisting the mountain climber — whose replies had to be distinctly heard — up out of sight just inside the proscenium arch. He was, if I remember rightly, tied on a wooden swing made fast to a convenient pipe. The crowd of tourists, all craning upward, gave the sense of a nearby height that the voice from on high emphasized. The single piece of scenery I had painted to suggest, somewhat in the Hokusai manner, the base of a cliff running up out of sight toward the invisible voice on its perch. Across the gaping void I strung the "cut-out" of a rustic fence, as though some one might conceivably fall off if he ventured beyond it. And behind that, to suggest height again, several cardboard silhouettes of the tops of rotund, cumulus clouds — these extravagant extras being magnanimously conceded by the management. There being no balcony at the Band Box and the tourists being well massed against the fence for most of the act, no eye in the audience saw enough of the board floor between the fence and the horizontal base of the clouds to shatter the illusion.

However, Sam Elliot, the producer, now Professor of Dramatics at Smith College, had his doubts on the subject. I returned to a rehearsal to find my single cliff laid flat on the floor in front of the fence as an additional masking piece. As soon as Sam left the building I set it up again as a cliff. At the next rehearsal it was flat on the stage as a shelf of rock. The exchange went on with the utmost regularity until just before the opening night when I set the piece up again as a cliff. And the curtain finally went up on it in that position.

II

I have dwelt on the details of that first assignment because they remain typical of the problems of scenic design in any so-called art theatre even after the stage floor can be cut, and the budget provides for as many pieces of scenery as one wants to use and a full crew to handle them. The mountain top in "Peer Gynt" was in many details more solid, but essentially as suggestive as the cliff at the Band Box. The distant ranges of Norwegian peaks were as summary as the outline of cumulus clouds. They were simply better scaled, more adroitly placed and gave an illusion more complete. The principle of design remained the same for the church in "The Failures"—the base of a Gothic column (without a Gothic moulding on it) placed well downstage to suggest to the audience's eye, and so make them feel, the mass they could not see; a shaft of light to suggest a window out of sight in the wings like the original man on the cliff; and again the railroad tracks in "Liliom" that seemed to go on for miles. The same principle applied to the judges' box of "From Morn to Midnight," with the seething arena of bicycle-race fans presumably in the blackness below, invisible but actual nevertheless; the Princess' ship in "Marco" which was very little more than the fretted stern silhouetted against the sky.

The problem has been summarized in Degas' dictum: You make a crowd with five people not with fifty: the problem of the suppression of unnecessary detail which any art student learns at his first life class while ostensibly trying to copy a nude model. The basic principle of scenic design is the truism which every worker in any graphic art accepts as his working hypothesis: the more one shows the less one reveals. Only elimination can produce expressive design whatever the scale of design be, within the borders of a rug, a picture frame or the frame of a stage itself. Even for a realistic script, Flaubert's advice to Maupassant holds good: one must note not all the documentary details, but the one significant detail, which will identify even so common an object as a white horse instantly and irrevocably. And finally, as proved by the cliff that stood first on one end and then on the other, one must work in fundamental agreement with the producer who is welding a production together and giving it its total impact on an audience.

None of the perennially advertised nostrums of scenic design have ever seemed to me important in themselves — nothing but costumes, nothing but light, no paint, nothing but flat decorative painting, not an atom of realism, realism *à l'outrance*, platforms, stairways, trestles, screens.

Significant form has become a recurrent phase in modern aesthetics. In the theatre any form may be significant. A few kitchen chairs from the nearest hardware store may be arranged, on the stage, in a design no less stylized than if every character were seated on a symbolic block of wood. The pattern of a wallpaper, in itself ugly and hideous, may be made the significant pattern of a setting, and its effect beautiful. Parts of any stage setting are inevitably facsimiles: actors must light cigars, strike matches, handle daggers, shoot guns, draw sabres, blow out candles, turn on electric lights. Due to the exigencies of the fact that the theatre does reproduce human action, there is no setting however symbolic or stylized that is not naturalistic or realistic in some of its details. There is no setting however realistic or naturalistic in its details that can be completely so. Theatrical art cannot be pure in the way that contemporary painting for a decade foolishly aspired to become. To cultivate any of the taboos current at one time or another since the modern scenic movement began, is to become a theatrical prude. Origins, as a philosopher once remarked, have nothing to do with values. What matters in stage design is not where things come from, but how they are used. Like the producer, the designer is dealing not with abstract categories of things, but with the functions of things that interact and interplay and make their effect as a whole: a cohesion of colors, lights, gestures, voices. The matter of style or art is not inherent in any of them, but in the way they cohere in their total impact.

Which is but another way of saying that stage design is part and parcel of the job of producing a play, of putting it across the footlights, of convincing or arousing an audience. The only single criterion is the way a particular producer has decided to interpret a play, the only test the psychology of a particular audience. There is no one way of designing any play because there is no one foreordained way of producing it.

Had Moeller instead of Komisarshevsky directed "The Tidings Brought to Mary," the design for the unit setting would have been totally different in quality and effect. And the same would have held true if Komisarshevsky instead of Moeller had staged "R. U. R." I could design the settings for the same play in succession for two different producers in two different types of theatres and the resulting designs would be totally different even though I started one set as soon as the other had gone to the carpenters to be built.

Moreover, no setting has any final quality except in conjunction with the kind of acting that takes place in front of it. Acting out of key with a setting can destroy its quality no less than a setting out of key with the action can damage a play. Robert Edmond Jones' stylized settings for "Macbeth" are usually spoken of as one of his rare failures: the failure lay in the fact that not an actor could sustain the mood they evoked or the interpretation that the production as a whole pretended to give. Had Tairov's actors played in them, every one would have seen these macabre skeletons of sets with entirely different eyes. They would actually have been different. Part of the comparative failure of "The Tidings Brought to Mary" resulted from the fact that the acting company were unable to sustain the mood of austere formalism of the platform setting that Komisarshevsky had conceived.

Finally, the anticipation of the type and temper of an audience, its habits of mind, its background, also determine the design of a setting. For the purpose of any production is to convince an audience of the reality of what it sees acted, and realism is only one way of making human experience real. To achieve that reality is the first business of any theatrical performance, whether the play deals with familiar types from around the corner, or legendary figures of 3000 B.C. or 2000 years hence. Until a performance achieves that immediate reality, no audience can identify itself sufficiently with the human beings on the stage to share their emotions or be interested in their experiences. "What's Hecuba to him, or he to Hecuba?" is a reflection that may profit the spectator on his way out after the final curtain. But if that skepticism assails him in the theatre, the production fails.

The function of stage scenery, and hence the job of the scene designer, is to help in creating that necessary reality of every production, to induce an audience, as soon as the curtain is up, to accept the world of the play and vicariously to live in it. Scenic design, as I've said elsewhere, aims to stimulate the kind of seeing which is believing.

The First Ten Years

III

For that reason it has been so essential a part of every Guild production from the outset. For the Guild's avowed purpose has always been to produce plays which, according to Broadway or the Backwoods, the public didn't want, to project convictions about human beings, the motives and incentives, the rewards and punishments of behavior, which were neither obvious nor easily acceptable; to give plays that were a step or two in advance of our accepted ideas, plays that actually combatted our current hazy or lazy notions about human nature, our rubber stamp notions of good and evil, our psychological stereotypes and taboos. In almost every case (though of course we have often enough made our mistakes and fallen back on the easy and the obvious) our audiences had to be won to a point of view, a conviction, a vision of life that was neither obvious at the outset nor that lay so far from the usual orbit of their conceptions that it was not easy to share.

The major share of transporting our audience to fresh fields and pastures new fell upon our directors and the actors. But in most of our productions the settings were of material help.

Liliom is a tough, as romantic as a quotation from Goethe. The toughs we know are skeptical and cynical. Nevertheless Molnar's hero was, to the Guild, not a sloppy and false piece of sentimentalism but alive with genuine insight. And the audience could share that insight if they could accept *Liliom* at the outset as racially different enough not to be ridiculous where the play began, and universal enough before the play ended to be understandable. For this reason the amusement park of the prologue was packed with as much local color as possible. It was as Hungarian as we could make it. The audience was transported to another world, and so inclined to accept a " bum " who did not act according to type. The park bench was invested with all the poetry of evening that theatrical gauze and theatrical lighting could give it. It was imbued with beauty, as though the barker and the slavey were Pelleas and Melisande. For they were genuinely in love. And unless a spell could be cast by that scene, unless an audience were actually convinced of that fact, the rest of the story would be rhetorical buncombe.

Josef Schildkraut brought intense conviction and enthusiasm to the role. He had acted the entire script in German for me and Ralph Roeder, then reading foreign plays for us, and held us spellbound to the last line. *Liliom* lived in him from the first. Eva Le Gallienne has probably never surpassed her interpretation of *Julie*. With it she " arrived." Dudley Digges made *The Sparrow* as unforgettable as *Jimmy Caesar*, which had originally established him overnight as one of the finest actors in the American theatre. And the script is of course the best that Molnar has ever written. The combination would undoubtedly have triumphed in any setting. But if the amusement park at the outset had looked like a travelling tent show at Elmira or Hoosick Corners, if the park had been painted on a flat backdrop and seemed, like so many stage landscapes, an enlarged colored chromo of the early nineties, they would have had a harder time of it.

The so-called Heaven scene of "Liliom" is another instance of how inextricably design is bound up with a producer's problems. *Liliom* finds himself before the bar of ultimate judgment, but, as the script indicates, he sees it as only one more police court, God as an examining magistrate and the attending angels as jailers. The script is vague as to just how obviously they are one or the other. Frank Reicher, as the producer, warned me that this scene was the making or breaking of the play. (It had failed everywhere in Europe even in Rhinehardt's hands in Berlin.) And he believed that part of the difficulty had been in every case, that this scene had been made too fantastic; attendants, half in uniform, half in trailing robes, sprouting concealed wings, or in uniform with palm leaves instead of sabres. The scene became burlesque, and according to Reicher the play was over. "Above everything," he warned me, "no Orpheus in the Underworld." We worried considerably about it and finally agreed that up to the level of *Liliom's* eye the scene was to be as tangibly a police court; God was to be in uniform like any local judge; the attendant angels like the police he had just left. Above that, somehow, heaven was to be suggested. I attempted this by cutting the walls of the courtroom at the wainscoting and taking off the ceiling;

the court became the skeleton of a room under an expanse of blue sky, obviously in heaven.

How much that had to do with the play's success neither Reicher nor I, of course, can ever know. But it did sustain the mood and the method of his production. The scene carried the audience with it, even though on the opening night, God forgot his lines, unceremoniously left the stage, got his cue from the prompter, returned to his seat, and, having picked up the wrong cue, began most of the scene over again.

However, Pitoëv's more recent production of "Liliom" was as phenomenally successful in Paris as the Guild's had been in New York. But his scene in heaven was deliberately fantastic, and the fair, the park, indeed every other scene in the play, as deliberately symbolic. Some day an astute millionaire will arrange an International Theatrical Congress, whose program will consist of nothing but the same play staged and acted successive nights by Rhinehardt, Pitoëv, Tairov, The Moscow Art Theatre, the Guild, and the leading theatres of Stockholm, Vienna and Prague. We should then learn a great deal more about production than we know now.

IV

"Liliom" can serve as a typical instance of what the business of scenic designing really means. And the few decisions I have cited are typical of twenty others that had to be made and seemed at the time equally momentous. The story could be substantially duplicated for every Guild production. The same choice of alternatives applies to the placing of doors and windows, chairs and tables, to every detail of costume and make-up, the length of a tunic, the cut of a wig, or the "props" which the actors handle — a dagger too long or a sword not conveniently hung may very easily spoil a crucial gesture. A table six inches too wide may jam a necessary bit of action which cannot take place elsewhere. A door too far downstage may make an important entrance invisible to a fourth of the audience. The producer must either see his way to restaging that entrance or the set must be redesigned. Scenery is usually thought of as being conceived primarily as a picture. A designer learns after a few years to spend most of his preliminary planning on the plan and structure of his set. Once that is geared to the general scheme of the production, color and ornament follow.

Producers differ greatly of course in the ability to visualize a production. Many of the most experienced have the haziest ideas as to the size of the limitations of even the simplest stage, the amount of furniture it can conveniently hold, or the space that even an approved design will give for the action planned. Producers like Komisarshevsky who conceive the general pictorial structure of a production with exactitude and are technically able to carry through even the lighting rehearsals, are the exception rather than the rule. But even in Komisarshevsky's case, his scheme for "The Tidings" was far more complete than his conception of "Peer Gynt." Often the designer brings ideas that help the director; and as often the director stimulates the designer. No producer that I have worked with has ever failed to design at least part of a production. The wheat field seen through the barn door of the last act of "The Power of Darkness" resulted from Emanuel Reicher's plea that somewhere the beauty of the outside world must break in on the moment of redemption. Most of the structure of "He Who Gets Slapped" grew out of Robert Milton's insistence that he must have a post or a column somewhere near the center of the stage about which to build certain "business." The brain storm in "The Adding Machine" was the result of a remark of Moeller's — "If the whole scene could go mad, blood you know, something to show what's happening inside the man . . ." — the sort of remark he characterized as inspirational after our electrician, Mike O'Connor, two electrical supply companies and myself had experimented for several weeks with gauzes, spot lights and revolving discs, and approximated his intuition. Indeed, it is Moeller's conviction that the number of such inspirational moments is far greater than either of us care to remember, and that he has actually designed most of my best settings although the routine of the theatre enables me to take credit for the result.

However, at its vaguest, the producer's eye is a stereopticon compared with that of the author, even after years of successful writing for the theatre. Bernard Shaw is probably the only living dramatist of importance who successfully visualizes his action in script. A designer may not hang all the pictures dictated by the stage directions in Roebuck's study in "Man and Superman," or rearrange the shrubbery in the Granada garden. But let him alter the positions of the doors and windows or so much as a single piece of furniture in the first act of "Heartbreak House" and the flow of action will be so seriously impeded that he will promptly have to put them back again exactly where Mr. Shaw placed them. But in studying most scripts these elementary questions have to be threshed out at the outset. Often all the furniture that an author calls for, if it were used, would so clutter the stage, that the characters could act the play only on condition of playing leapfrog at intervals. Often the setting according to the script is the worst possible arrangement for climactic moment.

Settings therefore start with a ground plan. The producer is principally concerned with his scheme of action, the grouping of his players, the general line of movement from one focal point to another. Once a working agreement is attained on that point, the designer — and this has become a Guild tradition — subject to the budget allotted him is left free as to almost all pictorial details, on the very sound assumption that only under these conditions can he achieve an expressive result.

The procedure is often less simple, for dramatists continue to write scripts which deliberately ignore the limitations of the theatre and the restricted space which they well know is all that even the most opulent producer (except in a few German theatres endowed by the State) can afford to rent or own. Even Mr. Shaw carelessly injects a Sphinx, a " baby Sphinx " to be sure, into one of the three swift scenes which open " Caesar and Cleopatra." The ancient expedient of painting the monument on the backdrop cannot be resorted to, because Cleopatra must be reclining asleep in its paws, and pop out of the shadow at a given moment. And Mr. Shaw like any other man of the theatre knows that nothing will break the spell of an act or breed a restless audience more quickly than long waits for scene shifting between short scenes. A succession of scene shifts will often weight the chances of success or failure by every 30 seconds. Consider the case of O'Neill in the first act of " Marco," beginning with a gigantic tree, and following with three ponderous samples of the architecture of Syria, Islam, India, winding up with nothing less than a gate in the wall of China, which after a five-minute scene must disappear instantly to reveal the palace of Kublai Khan.

In this age of mechanical marvels, there is not a device which can solve problems of this sort. The few mechanical aids to scene shifting invented by the Germans are so prohibitive in first cost in this country that no one could afford to install them even if the ground rent of cities did not restrict stage space to the point where there is no room for them. Mechanically our so-called modern stages are if anything more primitive than those of the Renaissance and the court theatres of the 18th century. Everything has to be done in the last analysis by hand. The weight of every piece of scenery is a crucial factor, for it effects the speed with which it can be moved and the number of men — with a wage scale mounting every year — required to handle it. The most beautiful set of scenery can wreck a play if it takes five minutes too long to shift, or requires a weekly payroll that can very easily eat up any possible margin of profit.

Perhaps it is just as well that playwrights demand the impossible and that modern mechanics does not untie every Gordian knot for the designer in the twinkling of an eye. Whatever mastery modern designers have achieved is due very largely to the limitations they have had to work under originally, small stages and inadequate budgets. As artists, simplicity was their natural creed, but it was a virtue fortified by necessity. Even though experimental theatres have prospered, the imagination of playwrights outstripped their larger stages and their ampler budgets. The demands of "Marco," "Back to Methuselah," or "Strange Interlude" continue the stimulating struggle with the limitations of space and time.

V

The Guild, nevertheless, in building its new theatre tried to contribute to improving the stage mechanically, in order to cramp directors and playwrights as little as possible.

Stage space cannot be constricted below a certain point without creating needless limitations. The shallow stages current in New York, 20 and 22 feet deep, flout even the minimum needs of the average play, make rehearsals a needlessly long agony for every one involved, and add, needlessly, to the production expense. Such stages are not necessary: they express merely the easiest way out on the part of speculative builders who give the least possible to speculative producers for the maximum possible rent. Despite a façade of pastry decorations the average New York stage had become as contemptuous of a decent minimum as any old style tenement.

The architectural scheme of the new Guild Theatre was evolved in order to break down the stale tradition that the stage had to be sacrificed for seating capacity, and that seating capacity could be attained only by rows one could hardly crawl through, and a lobby so small that patrons were all but shoved on the street during intermissions. Thanks to C. Howard Crane's ingenious adaptation of one of Norman Bel Geddes' theatre projects — with Geddes as consultant — the Guild stage is 20 feet deeper, the space between seats wider, the lobby space probably five times as great as the traditional theatre plan could achieve on the same plot of ground, and this without sacrifice of seating capacity originally planned.

The other contribution of the Guild toward the development of modern stage craft has been its consistent attempt from the first days at the Garrick to develop and perfect its lighting system. For the only new means that modern invention has given the stage is the magic of electric light. Its effect can be magical because it can be accurately directed (through spotlights) and controlled (by the dimmers of its switchboard) so that lamps can be slowly dimmed out or brought up full, subtly enough for the change to be imperceptible. The light plot of any play is equivalent to an orchestral accompaniment, and influences the spectator's mood more quickly and more directly than the color or the form of the set itself. If any director were given his choice between playing in front of bare curtains with a flexible and complete lighting equipment, or in a set lighted with an even and rigid glare, he would, I think, choose the first alternative. Certainly a designer would prefer a badly painted set and ample lighting equipment to a perfectly painted set and inadequate lights.

For under inadequate lighting the most beautifully painted set goes for nothing. The full value of any set, its form, color, its every accent and the mood it establishes and sustains, depends on the balance of light on it. The old method was to hang lamps in tin troughs and flood the scene with a uniform radiance. Such lighting was in fact technically known as flood lighting. It lighted the leading actor to be sure, but it lighted the buttons on the butler's uniform or the doorknob upstage with equal brilliance. The new method of lighting focuses a group of lights, different in color and intensity, on every part of the stage and thus modulates them continuously to emphasize the actor and underscore the action. The stage is full of pools of light carefully spotted over the stage, so angled and controlled that they are usually invisible until the actor walks in them, and so controlled that they can be raised or lowered, leaving their emphasis if necessary only on a single face or a single chair.

To do this enough lights are needed and an elaborate system of control. No play can be lighted unless there are enough lamps to spot everything — as many as half a dozen are sometimes needed to cover a single scene on a couch, and half a dozen more different in color and intensity to light its immediate surroundings. If one cannot change that intensity and control one by one, no change can be made that is not a visible jump completely disconcerting to the spectator.

When we began at the Garrick we had no equipment to speak of. The tradition survived that almost anything would do to light a play once the scenery and costumes were paid for. The notion that every lamp had to be individually controlled was looked upon as nothing short of madness. Nevertheless, the indispensable Mike O'Connor — our stage electrician and the one member of our original stage crew who is still with us — Monroe Pevear, and I persisted. Before we moved to the Guild we had achieved a standard of equipment so that the color of the sky could be changed almost instantly, to almost any point of the spectrum, and a hundred "spots," if necessary, were available for any production. When we moved to the Guild Theatre we added a new type of switchboard to control them more flexibly. Unfortunately not a single American manufacturer could meet our original specifications. But they were partially met, and the control of stage lighting pushed a step forward.

Today as from the first the light rehearsals are as important as any others in the preparation of a play. If the actors cannot give up the stage during the day it is the unwritten rule that the designer sits up all night with the stage electrician to get an act ready for the company next morning. And the light rehearsals continue night after night if necessary. At a directors' rehearsal the lights are watched and criticized as carefully as is the acting. For a large production, the last rehearsal is Sunday morning when the light plot is run through on an actorless stage until it is reasonably certain to go without a hitch. Any slips or mistakes occurring at the Sunday night dress rehearsal are corrected and rehearsed again Monday before the public opening. My fellow directors have disputed any number of my contentions in regard to both the theory and practice of stage setting; they have never disputed the necessity of ample lighting equipment. When every expenditure was a crucial one at the Garrick, every cent that could be spared went into building up our permanent installation. Today, no matter how high crew expenses during a rehearsal have run, there is never any question of curtailing a light rehearsal until the result satisfies the six of us.

VI

That, in outline, is what setting the stage at the Guild amounts to. Our contribution to modern design has, of course, not been unique: it has sustained the same tradition carried on elsewhere by such American designers as Robert Edmond Jones, Norman Bel Geddes, Mordekai Gorelik, Raymond Sovey, Cleon Throckmorton, Aline Bernstein, and Jo Mielziner — the last five having achieved some of their most important settings for Guild productions. Guild productions over a decade have helped to establish the fact that stage setting is an essential, and often vital part, of the art of the modern theatre. It will remain so insofar as the Guild continues to find experimental material and to face the necessity of bringing audiences into contact with new experiences and unfamiliar worlds.

THE LITTLE THEATRE GROWS UP

By Lawrence Langner

The Washington Square Players in the year 1914, produced a program of one-act plays in the little Band Box Theatre, seating 299 persons; its direct lineal descendant, the Theatre Guild, in the year 1929, is providing ten of the large cities in the United States with a program of from five to six artistic plays of the kind not ordinarily produced in the commercial theatre, acted by some of the best acting talent available in the country, and running for seasons of from 5 to 15 weeks outside New York, to a full season of 30 weeks in New York itself. I shall try to trace the steps of internal development which have made possible the growth of the Guild to an art theatre conducted on an unusually extensive scale, and to explain some of the principles which I believe to be entirely new in the history of the theatre, and which have been utilized by the Guild in its development as a group organization.

Other members of the Guild Board have explained their

The Theatre Guild

special provinces in the Guild, which have brought its artistic and organization activities to its present stage of development. I shall deal here with the particular work in which I have been largely engaged — the planning of the Guild's future development — which work, like all the other activities of the Guild Board, has always been in the nature of a collaboration with the other five Guild directors.

The Theatre Guild began with an idea which was in my mind, as well as in the minds of a number of others, after the demise of the Washington Square Players. It was that the little theatre should grow up. The Theatre Guild, both in its inception and in its subsequent development, has always embodied this idea, and it is in this respect that the Theatre Guild has differed from the dozens of other art theatres in this country and abroad, which have been satisfied to remain in the little theatre stage.

The beginnings of the Washington Square Players were humble indeed, far more humble than the beginnings of the Theatre Guild; for when we started the Theatre Guild we had behind us the experiences of the Washington Square Players. Nevertheless, it was in the work of the Washington Square Players that the germs of many of the ideas now forming a basic part of the Guild policy were developed. Notwithstanding this, the Washington Square Players was in every sense a little theatre, despite the fact that it occupied the Comedy Theatre in New York City after its brief sojourn at the Band Box. It was a splendid training ground for writers, actors, producers and scenic artists, for its efforts were made on a scale which enabled the beginner to sustain his particular work. The young playwright who did not possess the strength or depth necessary for the production of a long play, furnished one-act plays which were perfectly sustained for twenty minutes; the young actor who could not sustain a characterization throughout a long play was able to triumph in a leading part in a short play; the scenic artist had greater scope and variety than in the larger theatre, since at least four sets, each in a different locale, were required for each evening's bill of one-act plays; the producer had an equal chance, and without the risks of failure which follow in the wake of heavier productions. In spite of all these advantages, the Washington Square Players were not satisfied with the production of short plays. Like all children, they longed to grow up. Even in their infancy, they attempted to produce one of the most difficult of the modern plays, Chekov's "The Seagull." It was a disastrous failure, and taught us the lesson that we could not run before we could walk.

The earliest productions of the Players might be described as those of superior amateurs, without bringing the flush of indignation to the cheek of any one involved in the proceedings, or without in any way slurring the amateur. The standards of acting were about on the level obtaining in little theatres today, except in those where strictly professional companies are employed. Later, the company was strengthened by some sterling actors. The

Players opened a side door into the theatre, and through it came an array of new talent; the producing talents of Goodman and Moeller, the scenic talents of Simonson and Peters, the acting talents of the artists already named, and a host of others. On the playwrighting side, the reckoning was not so good. Nevertheless, a number of the Washington Square Players' authors have written long plays, but this has not been the chief contribution of the group.

The period in which the Players came to life was a very vital one in the theatre; it not only witnessed this group movement, which absorbed a great deal of the amateur impetus; it was also the period when the Provincetown Players, headed by George Cram Cook, came into being and cradled the early works of O'Neill and Susan Glaspell. This theatre was always a more personal expression of the authors behind it, than was the Washington Square Players group, with the result that it tended to develop its authors rather than its audiences; a worthy and important aim, difficult to achieve, and deserving of the greatest praise. The Provincetown Players were frankly experimental when the Washington Square Players were attempting to produce plays which would be in healthy competition with the plays of Broadway. The Washington Square Players joined the issue of the Art Theatre versus the Commercial Theatre; it sought to produce its plays at the Comedy Theatre in competition with commercial attractions; it sent a travelling company on tour; and it produced Ibsen's "Ghosts," and Shaw's "Mrs. Warren's Profession," but

The First Ten Years

without the success which the efforts merited. The war put a stop to its activities before it had grown strong enough to stand on its own feet.

In addition to the experience which was gained in this group, the Players contributed at least two extremely valuable organization methods, and an extremely valuable artistic method, all of which were later to be of great importance to the Guild. It inaugurated the operation of a theatre under the direction of a Board of Managers, which performed the general function of controlling the artistic and financial policies of the theatre, the work of the Board not only including the selection of the plays but also the selection of the theatre, the actors, the director, and the scenic artist to be employed in each production, so that the direction of the organization was centered entirely in the Board, while the various executives designated by the Board carried out the policies which were agreed upon. This system has been the basis of the Guild's directorate. The Washington Square Players also developed a method of play production, under the supervision of its Board of Managers, which, so far as I know, was not used by any theatre before it, but was eminently successful both with the Washington Square Players and, with modifications, with the Theatre Guild. Special rehearsals of each play are given before the Board of Managers during successive stages of the period of rehearsal, and after the rehearsal is over and the actors leave the theatre, the director and the Board have a conference, at which the various notes

The Theatre Guild

made by the Board members are submitted. Each point in the production is examined and argued until a conclusion is reached, the Board having the final say in any dispute.

Another organization method which the Guild inherited from the Washington Square Players was that of securing a membership audience, the members of which subscribe in advance for a series of plays, their subscriptions furnishing the organization with some of the funds necessary to produce the plays. This subscription method, having been adopted and greatly improved upon, has resulted in the Guild's extensive definite supporting membership of over 60,000 members throughout the country. These members, by paying for their seats in advance, provide a guarantee against too great a loss on each production, which makes a subsidy unnecessary. The number of members obtained by the Washington Square Players by means of its subscription list was, however, never quite large enough to keep the group out of debt, so that the subscription system did not realize the same success with the Players as with the Guild, and financial help in the way of private subsidy was often necessary in the earlier group.

During the war, after the group was dispersed, the dramatic critic in one of the New York papers, commenting upon the failure of the Washington Square Players, made some slurring remarks, which caused me to write a letter to him in the month of June, 1918, from which I quote the following:

The First Ten Years

"The Washington Square Players are no more dead than any other organization that is marking time on account of the War. The dramatic impulse which created it and kindred organizations is a living, breathing, real thing, much more alive than those who sneer at us.

"The doctors and wiseacres of Broadway and the newspaper offices who are busy analyzing the causes of the 'death' of the Washington Square Players, must not be surprised if the corpse expresses its appreciation by registering a vigorous kick."

I had at that time resolved that as soon as the war was over, I would make an effort to reorganize the group, though upon a somewhat different basis. When the War came to an end, I suggested to Philip Moeller and Helen Westley that we should immediately start to work to create a new art theatre, and, backed by their enthusiasm, I wrote letters to a number of former members of the Washington Square Players, inviting them to attend a meeting at the home of Miss Josephine A. Meyer, who had been one of the prominent members of the Washington Square Players, and whose spirit had been a source of inspiration to us all. Miss Meyer was ill at the time, but it seemed fitting that our first meeting should be in her home, always a sanctuary of artistic faith and idealism.

Josephine Meyer was not to live long after this meeting, but I like to think that her spirit has always been with the Guild. In spite of her weakened condition, she bravely undertook the duties of one of the Guild's play readers.

The atmosphere of our first meeting, which I well

remember, was one of the greatest enthusiasm. We not only discussed the forming of an art theatre, we discussed very fully the kind of art theatre which we wanted to form. It is a tribute to the spirit and intelligence which characterized the discussion at this meeting, when I say that the conclusions which were set in writing after the meeting, have formed the Magna Charta of the Theatre Guild, and have never been departed from in principle. For the benefit of those who are interested in the conclusions which were reached at the end of this first meeting of the Guild, I quote the following which I noted down in a letter written directly after the meeting:

"1.— That we would form a group to carry out the idea of an expert theatre; that is, a theatre which would be entirely different from the Little Theatre or Provincetown Players type of theatre, but would be made up only of artists of the theatre who are experts in their work.

"2.— That we would either lease or secure the building of a theatre seating a considerable number of people, and certainly larger than the usual Little Theatre (between 500 and 600 seating capacity), in some place where the rents were sufficiently low not to make rentals a burden.

"3.— To govern absolutely by a committee which will delegate its executive and administrative powers to members thereof."

After these policies had been formulated, a great many discussions took place at meetings which were held at the homes of Philip Moeller and myself. I remember that Lee

The First Ten Years

Simonson, with his own eager enthusiasm for the theatre, called upon me one afternoon to discuss ways and means of starting the new theatre. He spent the afternoon with me. I invited him to dinner. He spent all evening arguing with me, staying until two o'clock in the morning. It was then too late for him to go home, so I put him up for the night. He got up early the next morning, and continued arguing until lunch. I made my point, but we both almost lost our minds.

Notwithstanding the thorough discussions which took place before we started work on the Guild's first productions, the principles which were outlined at the original meeting of the Guild were adhered to throughout all further discussions, and it was finally decided to go ahead with the engagement of expert actors, in accordance with paragraph one of the conclusions at the first meeting; to secure the Garrick Theatre, in accordance with paragraph two of our conclusions; and to form a Board of Managers which would delegate its executive and administrative powers to the members of the group, as outlined in the third paragraph.

Whereas the earlier theatre had proven to be a splendid training ground for the amateur, this new theatre was to be an adult theatre, attempting the highest expressions of the theatrical art, and using the finest talent available in the theatre for its avowed purpose, which, like that of the Washington Square Players, was to produce plays of artistic merit not ordinarily

The Theatre Guild

produced by the commercial managers. The group invited a number of well-known players who were sympathetic toward the art theatre movement to join the Guild, and with a company composed largely of players recruited from the ranks of the commercial theatre, with a few amateurs to fill in where professionals were not available, the performances of the two long plays of the Guild's initial season were given. The Guild, thus launched in its program, has never departed from this policy. It has produced the masterpieces of many countries, and has always attempted to do this with the best acting talent it could procure in the American theatre.

What is there in this policy which makes it a desirable policy for an art theatre to pursue — or which justifies any recommendation of such a policy to others? At first glance it seems clear that the work of the earlier Washington Square Players, in developing new talent, was of considerably greater importance than the work of the Guild in utilizing talent already in existence. Indeed, since it was the Players which developed, in the main, the young talents of the Theatre Guild group, it is obvious that, without the earlier work of the Players, the Guild could not have existed at all, just as a promising athlete could not become a football player without first learning the game. The earlier Players group had served its purpose; it had acted as the incubator for several talents in the theatre. These talents were not teaching talents; if they had been, the Players might still be in existence, turning amateur actors into professional actors, and so forth. They were producing talents, and when the step of using the best actors available in the theatre, and the forming of a company of such actors was decided upon, the Guild pushed the whole cause of the art theatre into the vanguard of American cultural life by showing that artistic plays, when well-acted, were as interesting, and indeed, more interesting, than the rubbish which had passed for theatrical fare just before and during the war. In other words, instead of making the artistic play bear the brunt of bad acting performances and bad productions, as had commonly been the case with so-called "high-brow" efforts, the Guild realized that great plays needed great performances, and set out to secure them. It lost to a certain extent, the capacity for experiment with raw material in acting talent. Indeed, it lost the general capacity for experiment which marked the first phase of the group, but it gained a competence in performances and production which won an audience away from the "commercial" theatre; an audience which we confidently hope will continue to support the Guild so long as it continues in the policy of producing great plays, greatly acted and sensitively produced.

In our early days in the Garrick Theatre, the Guild was building upon a sound artistic policy and a sound economic policy. We had gone a step forward in the production of artistic plays with the best professional talent we could secure in the commercial theatre. We had accepted the challenge of Broadway, and had put these plays into direct competition with the Broadway theatre, with full confidence that there was an audience eagerly awaiting such plays, a confidence which has since been justified up to the hilt. We had gone a step further in our development of the subscription methods of the Players group, and had also developed a policy of using the Garrick as an incubator house in which we hatched the plays which were later transferred to a Broadway theatre. We were dissatisfied, however, with the fact that, like the other managers on Broadway, we cast each play with a different group of actors, many of whom had never played together before. In many instances this had proven unsatisfactory, for in "casting to type," we sometimes had to employ actors who had never appeared with us before, with the result that we were often uncertain as to these actors' capabilities, and found our mistakes to be disastrous on opening night.

The Moscow Art Theatre visited the United States in the year 1925 and gave us an unforgettable demonstration of the extraordinary value of an Acting Company. I and some of the other members of the Guild Board had conferences with Stanislavsky in regard to the possibility of his coöperating with the Guild in the formation of a Guild Acting Company, but the plan failed to materialize. We realized, however, that the Guild had outgrown the plan of incubating plays in the Garrick and transferring them to other theatres, and that for the future development of our artistic policy, we needed a theatre which was large enough to hold the scenery of more than one production, so that we might have more than one play running in the theatre at the same time, presented by an Acting Company appearing in repertory, and developing ensemble acting performances along the lines of the Moscow Art Theatre.

The Guild Theatre was built to house this idea, giving equal importance to the artistic problems of the theatre, and to the housing of the subscription audience. During the first year of our occupancy of the Guild Theatre, we were busy overcoming the difficulties which followed upon our operating on a larger scale, and we continued to produce plays with actors recruited from Broadway until the end of this season. It was jokingly said at this time that our Acting Company consisted of Helen Westley. The nucleus of our Acting Company, however, had already appeared, since, during the years which preceded our occupancy of the Guild, we had been subjecting the acting talent available to us to a winnowing process, as the result of which such actors as Henry Travers and Dudley Digges had already appeared in a considerable number of Guild productions. It may be said with some truth that so long as we had a succession of failures we had an Acting Company, because our actors appeared in one part after another in quick succession, whereas when we produced a successful play, these actors were likely to be kept employed in that play for an entire season.

It seemed at this time that the next step in furthering the artistic aims of the Guild lay in the formation of an

Acting Company appearing in repertory. When we came to investigate the question of repertory, however, we encountered difficulties which, after giving them mature consideration, made us feel that the European system of repertory (changing the play each night) was not practical for us. Among these difficulties may be mentioned the excessive labor costs, due to changing the scenery each night, and perhaps the most serious objection, that the authors themselves were unwilling to make the sacrifice consequent upon giving their play only one or two evenings a week, even if the play remained in the repertory of the Acting Company for a number of years.

All these difficulties made us realize the necessity for a different policy which would give us some, at least, of the advantages of repertory without the disadvantages which were pointed out above. This resulted in our development of what has been termed the alternating system of repertory, which we put into operation for the season of 1926–27. Briefly stated, this system consists in running a play for a week at a time, and then changing the cast of that play into another play for the succeeding week, thus enabling us to use the Acting Company in more than one play at a time. As a variant of this system, we have even used one company in three plays, playing these plays each a week at a time.

The advantages of the alternating system, both from the artistic and the economic standpoint, are as follows:

The First Ten Years

1. The actors play a different part each week, so that their performances do not become mechanical, and they are relieved of the monotony of the long-run system;

2. It is possible for the Guild to secure good actors who are willing to appear in minor parts one week, provided they play better parts in the following week, this resulting in a very greatly improved acting ensemble;

3. Since the actors employed in one play also have to appear in another play, their versatility is developed, and the interest which is attached to one performance is carried over to the other;

4. Since the play is changed but once a week, the labor costs are not excessive, as compared with European repertory;

5. Since each play is given every other week, it insures a long run of the play, in point of time. There are two weeks of box office sale for each playing week. It has been found, strangely enough, that the weekly gross business done by a play under the alternating system compares favorably with the business done when the play is given a steady run;

6. It has enabled the Guild to use its best actors and actresses in a number of plays each season;

7. When the plays are sent on tour, each part of the Acting Company is enabled to play two or more plays, this reducing the travelling expense as compared with sending two or three companies each playing a single play.

The Theatre Guild

The disadvantages are as follows:

1. A certain amount of inflexibility;
2. The problem of having two plays in which the cast can readily alternate;
3. Slightly increased expenses;
4. Problems in advertising.

All in all, it is my opinion that the artistic advantages of this system far outweigh the disadvantages. While the first play given under the alternating plan failed to win popular approval, it was nevertheless a *succes d'estime*. The second play was eminently successful, and thereafter, for a period of nearly two years, each play given by the Guild under the alternating system was uniformly successful. Indeed, the proportion of the Guild's artistic failures was never so low as when the alternating system was in fullest operation in New York, during the seasons of 1926-27 and 1927-28. A tremendous improvement was seen in the quality of acting in the members of the Guild Acting Company, as each actor was given the opportunity of appearing in at least two or three roles each season.

I will digress for a moment to point out that the progression of the Guild, both in its economic and its artistic policy, has been in a series of steps, and that these steps have been such that the artistic policy was firmly established upon an economic basis before it was finally adopted. We had learned early in our history that what was best artistically was best economically. This turned out to be true of the alternating plan, for by enabling us to employ our best actors in a series of plays throughout the season, we were able to give these plays with the most distinguished talent available to us, keeping our company together and developing their ensemble work. This policy continued during our next season, and was the foundation of the next step in the Guild's development, that is, its seasons in other cities.

The fact that, as a result of our alternating plan, we had a group of actors able to give a series of plays one week after another at the end of our 1926–27 season, enabled us to give a short season of repertory in Chicago at the invitation of Mr. and Mrs. Insull. The great success of this season, and the tremendous demand on the part of audiences in other cities which we visited on our way to and from Chicago, made us realize that there was a keen desire for our plays outside New York by an audience which was as great as if not greater than the audience in New York itself. By the end of our season of 1928, we were in a position to divide our acting company into two groups, sending out one group in alternation in " Arms and the Man " and " The Guardsman," and the other group alternating " Marco Millions " and " Volpone." The alternating plan made it possible for us to send our best acting talent in these plays, and to tour with such heavy productions as " Marco Millions " and " Volpone," since it reduced the travelling expenses to one-half of what would have been the cost had we sent separate companies.

The Theatre Guild

The Guild's first year on a national scale, as was the case with its first year at the Guild Theatre, produced a whole crop of new problems, and because of these, it was found impossible to maintain the policy of alternation in New York, with so many members of our acting company on tour at the beginning of the season. We therefore reverted during the season of 1928-29 to our earlier method, while marking time to evolve a policy which would provide both New York and a number of other cities with plays given in alternation and coördinated on the basis of an ensemble acting company. This plan we will make an effort to put into effect during the season of 1929-30. Briefly stated, it involves the enlargement of our acting company to such a size that we are able to return to a policy of alternation, both in New York and other cities.

Alternation is not without its disadvantages, however, and one of these is the fact that it is sometimes difficult to find plays which fit into a program and are suitable for alternation. It also often happens that the Guild wishes to produce a play like "Porgy," employing a colored cast, or a play like "Wings Over Europe," employing an all-male cast. To give its program sufficient elasticity, alternation will probably be confined to four out of the six plays produced by the Guild during each season, while the two other plays may be cast according to their special requirements. It remains to be seen whether this program of "alternation," with such modifications as experience will bring, will form a final working system for an art theatre which is conducted on a far larger scale than has ever been attempted before.

Of one thing I feel certain — that if this system is successful in operation, it will mark the limit of the Guild's ability to maintain a general standard of artistic excellence in its work. It may even be necessary to reduce the number of cities in which the Guild's productions are made, if it is found to be impossible to provide all of them with Guild productions equal to the standards which we have set ourselves. I cannot see a future beyond that which I have briefly outlined here. I doubt the Guild's ability to produce more than six or seven plays each year. This sets the limit to what the Guild can accomplish on a national scale, except insofar as the electro-photographic reproduction of such work as we may produce in the theatre, can make a limited number of plays available to the large audiences of the motion picture houses.

Our experience with the Guild Repertory Company, which has toured in a large number of small cities in the United States, has led me to believe that the dissipation of energy caused by attempting to paint on too large a canvas makes it impossible to maintain in such a company the artistic standards which are required for the cultivation of public taste to an appreciation of good plays. That we may feel the need for satisfying the desire for artistic plays on the part of theatre audiences in these smaller cities, and may again attempt to solve this problem, is not without the bounds of possibility, but I think that our efforts in that direction may well take the form of organizing other Boards of Managers, functioning similarly to our own, which would take care of and be responsible for the Guild productions in such territories. For ourselves, I feel that with the establishment and maintenance of Guild seasons in seven or eight of the larger cities, the work of continuing to maintain the Guild standards of play selection and production at their highest will be sufficiently arduous to cause each and every one of us to write "Enough!"

One of the most interesting of the Guild's activities has been its organization of its audience. Beginning with the idea that there was an audience which was eager for good plays in New York, and discovering later on, against the contrary opinions expressed by many, that there were audiences equally eager outside New York, the Guild set about systematically to unite itself with its audience in such a way that the Guild now consists of those who produce the play and those who go to see the play. I think it can be safely said that the most important bond which exists between our audience and ourselves is the mutual interest in the production of plays of an unusual character presented with the greatest possible resources of the theatre. We have often noticed that our greatest support has come when we have made some unusually daring experiment, and especially an experiment which involves considerable financial loss, with very little likelihood of recouping it. Our production of "Back to Methuselah" is a case in point. I remember when I first visited Bernard Shaw in London, and arranged with him that the Guild should produce his plays in America, that I asked him for a contract in order that we might produce "Back to Methuselah." "A contract is quite unnecessary," said Shaw. "It is quite unlikely that another lunatic will want to put on the play." Several years later, Eugene O'Neill handed me the manuscript of "Strange Interlude" while I was on a visit to Bermuda. He informed me that he had already promised the manuscript to another manager who would produce it in case a well-known actress was willing to appear in it. I waited with a great deal of trepidation upon the verdict of this other manager. Fortunately for the Guild, he refused it, and the Guild produced the play purely in the spirit of experiment, fully intending to risk a considerable financial loss in the event that the play proved a failure from the popular standpoint. Both "Back to Methuselah" and "Strange Interlude" proved to be artistic successes of the first water, and the financial losses on the former were more than made up by the earnings of the latter.

While the enjoyment of belonging to an organization which has always been willing to take a chance in the direction of good plays has had a great deal to do with the building of the Guild membership, there have been other factors, such as its consideration for the comfort and convenience of the audience, which has been strangely lacking in the world of the theatre during the past 25 years. The Guild's seating methods, by which members receive their tickets by mail and are seated in regular seats, and the elimination of the ticket agency nuisance, are among the factors which have helped to sustain the Guild membership. In addition, the "Theatre Guild Magazine," under the editorship of Hiram Kelley Motherwell, has of late served as an organ to focus the attention of Guild members to all that is worthwhile that is going on in the theatre, whether this is by the Guild or by other managements. The evolution of the "Guild Magazine" from a four-folder sheet, which was originally written entirely by myself, into a small magazine, published quarterly, under the title of "The Theatre Guild Quarterly," into a magazine of some 80 pages, published monthly, with a circulation of over 50,000, is an indication of how the Guild, in building up its audience, has reached out in new directions to stimulate a general interest in the art of the theatre.

There is one great, crying need for the Guild Board itself. It is the need of always attempting the production of something a little more difficult than has been attempted before. The Guild's Board receives its greatest stimulus when attempting tasks which are more difficult than those which it has already accomplished. After producing "Strange Interlude," it seeks restlessly for another test of itself. So long as this spirit continues in our organization, I do not fear either stagnation or satiation.

APPENDIX

CASTS OF THE THEATRE GUILD SUBSCRIPTION PRODUCTIONS

First Season

BONDS OF INTEREST

by JACINTO BENAVENTE

*Translated by John Garrett Underhill
Staged by Philip Moeller
Settings and Costumes by Rollo Peters
Garrick Theatre, April 19, 1919*

Leander	Rollo Peters
Crispin	Augustin Duncan
Innkeeper	C. Hooper Trask
First Servant	Michael Carr
Second Servant	John Wilson
Harlequin	Walter Geer
Captain	Charles Macdonald
Maria	Beatrice Wood
Dona Sirena	Helen Westley
Columbine	Edna St. Vincent Millay
Laura	Kate Morgan
Risela	Mary Blair
Polichinelle	Dudley Digges
Wife of Polichinelle	Amelia Somerville
Silvia	Helen Freeman
Pantaloon	Leon Cunningham
Doctor	Henry Herbert
Secretary	Paul Lane
Constable	Jose Madrones

JOHN FERGUSON

by St. John Ervine

Staged by Augustin Duncan
Settings by Rollo Peters
Garrick Theatre, May 12, 1919

John Ferguson	Augustin Duncan
Sarah Ferguson	Helen Westley
Andrew Ferguson	Rollo Peters
Hannah Ferguson	Helen Freeman
James Caesar	Dudley Digges
Henry Withrow	Gordon Burby
Clutie	Henry Herbert
Sam Mawthinney	Walter Geer
Sergeant	Michael Carr

Second Season

THE FAITHFUL

by JOHN MASEFIELD

Staged by Augustin Duncan
Settings and Costumes by Lee Simonson
Garrick Theatre, Oct. 13, 1919

Asano	Rollo Peters
Kurano	Augustin Duncan
Hazana	Henry Travers
Kodera	Robert Donaldson
Hara	Erskine Sanford
An Old Samurai	W. J. Nelson
A Widow's Son	Noel Leslie
Shoda	Walter Geer
Kira	Henry Herbert
Sagisaka	Boris Korlin
Kamai	Walter Howe
Honzo	Erskine Sanford
Envoy	Henry Stillman
Ono	Milton Pope
Captain	Albert Lester
Lady Kurano	Helen Westley
Chikara	Richard Abbott
Starblossom	Julia Adler

THE RISE OF SILAS LAPHAM

Dramatized from Howells' Novel
by LILLIAN SABINE

Staged by Philip Moeller
Settings and Costumes by Lee Simonson
Garrick Theatre, Nov. 25, 1919

Silas Lapham	James K. Hackett
Bartley Hubbard	Milton Pope
Persis Lapham	Grace Henderson
Katie	Nell Hamilton
Milton Rogers	Henry Stillman
Penelope	Majorie Vonnegut
Irene	Grace Knell
Tom Corey	Noel Leslie
Anna Corey	Helen Westley
Bromfield Corey	Walter Howe
Nanny Corey	Mary Blair
Lily Corey	Grace Ade
Ethel Kingsbury	Mildred Keats
Mrs. Henry Bellingham	Nell Hamilton
Charles Bellingham	Richard Abbott
Mrs. James Bellingham	Sara Enright
James Bellingham	William Nelson
Mr. Sewell	Erskine Sanford
Mrs. Sewell	Mary True
Mr. Seymour	Robert Donaldson
Robert Chase	Walter Geer
Mr. Dunham	Henry Travers

POWER OF DARKNESS

by LEO TOLSTOI

Staged by Emanuel Reicher
Settings and Costumes by Lee Simonson
Garrick Theatre, Jan. 19, 1920

Peter	Henry Stillman
Anisya	Ida Rauh
Akoulina	Majorie Vonnegut
Nan	Maud Brooks
Nikita	Arthur Hohl
Akim	Frank Reicher
Matryona	Helen Westley
Marina	Bertha Broad
Mitrich	Erskine Sanford
First Neighbor	Nell Hamilton
Second Neighbor	Grace Ade
Simon	William Nelson
First Girl	Grace Knell
Second Girl	Mary True
Driver	Robert Donaldson
Bridegroom	Walter Geer
Ivan	Henry Travers
Best Man	Michael Carr
Matchmaker	Harrison Dowd
Police Officer	Richard Abbott
Elder	Milton Pope

JANE CLEGG

by St. John Ervine

Staged by Emanuel Reicher
Settings by Lee Simonson
Garrick Theatre, Feb. 23, 1920

Henry Clegg	Dudley Digges
Jane Clegg	Margaret Wycherly
Johnnie	Russell Hewitt
Jennie	Jean Bailey
Mrs. Clegg	Helen Westley
Mr. Morrison	Erskine Sanford
Mr. Munce	Henry Travers

THE DANCE OF DEATH

by AUGUST STRINDBERG

Condensed by Henry Stillman
Staged by Emanuel Reicher
Settings by Lee Simonson
Special performances, Garrick Theatre, May 9 and 20, 1920

Edgar	Albert Perry
Alice	Helen Westley
Judith	Pauline Polk
Curt	Dudley Digges
Allan	Robert Donaldson
Jenny	Valerie Stevens
Old Woman	Mary Paleologue
Lieutenant	Walter Geer

Third Season

THE TREASURE

by DAVID PINSKI

Translated by Ludwig Lewisohn
Staged by Emanuel Reicher
Settings by Lee Simonson
Garrick Theatre, Oct. 4, 1920

Chone, the Grave-Digger	Dudley Digges
Jachne-Braine, his Wife	Helen Westley
Tille, their Daughter	Celia Adler
Judke, their Son	Fred Eric
The Marriage Broker	Edgar Stehli
Soskin	Henry Travers
The President of the Community	Erskine Sanford
Members of the Society for Providing Dowries for Poor Maidens	William Rothschild
	Jacob Weiser
Members of the Society for the Care of the Sick	S. Karrakis
	Anthony Jochim
A Lawyer	Edwin Knopf
An Hysterical Woman	Lian Stephana
An Old Woman	Rolla Lyons
A Young Woman	Mary McAndrews
Her Little Daughter	Florence Curran
A Girl	Valerie Stevens
A Woman	Adelina Thomason
Another Woman	Edith Leighton
A Young Man	Saul Michaels
Another Man	William Worthington

HEARTBREAK HOUSE

by BERNARD SHAW

Staged by Dudley Digges
Settings by Lee Simonson
Garrick Theatre, Nov. 10, 1920

Ellie Dunn	Elizabeth Risdon
Nurse Guinness	Helen Westley
Captain Shotover	Albert Perry
Lady Utterword	Lucille Watson
Hesione Hushabye	Effie Shannon
Mazzini Dunn	Erskine Sanford
Hector Hushabye	Fred Eric
Boss Mangan	Dudley Digges
Randall Utterword	Ralph Roeder
The Burglar	Henry Travers

JOHN HAWTHORNE

by DAVID LIEBOVITZ

Staged by Philip Moeller
Settings by Sheldon K. Viele
Garrick Theatre (Matinees), Jan. 23, 1921

Henry Smart	Eugene Ordway
Joe Phoenix	Robert Babcock
Laura Smart	Muriel Starr
Ace Rogers	Edgar Stehli
Jim Farrell	Philip Wood
George	George Frenger
John Hawthorne	Warren Krech
First Acrobat	William Franklin
Second Acrobat	Bert Young
Judge	Franklyn Hanna
A Man	Jacob Weiser
Helen Macey	Lian Stephana
A Girl	Camille Pastorfield
Phil Boyerson	Edgar Kent

MR. PIM PASSES BY

by A. A. M**ILNE**

Staged by Philip Moeller
Settings by Lee Simonson
Garrick Theatre, Feb. 28, 1921

Anne	Peggy Harvey
Carraway Pim	Erskine Sanford
Dinah	Phyllis Povah
Brian Strange	Leonard Mudie
Olivia Marden	Laura Hope Crews
George Marden, J. P.	Dudley Digges
Lady Marden, his Aunt	Helen Westley

LILIOM

by FERENC MOLNAR

Staged by Frank Reicher
Settings and Costumes by Lee Simonson
Garrick Theatre, April 20, 1921

Marie	Hortense Alden
Julie	Eva Le Gallienne
Mrs. Muskat	Helen Westley
"Liliom"	Joseph Schildkraut
Four Servant Girls	Frances Diamond
	Margaret Mosier
	Anne de Chantal
	Elizabeth Parker
Policemen	Howard Claney
	Lawrence B. Chrow
Captain	Erskine Sanford
Plainclothes Man	Gerald Stopp
Mother Hollunder	Lilian Kingsbury
"The Sparrow"	Dudley Digges
Wolf Berkowitz	Henry Travers
Young Hollunder	William Franklin
Linzman	Willard Bowman
First Mounted Policeman	Edgar Stehli
Second Mounted Policeman	George Frenger
The Doctor	Robert Babcock
The Carpenter	George Frenger
First Policeman of the Beyond	Erskine Sanford
Second Policeman of the Beyond	Gerald Stopp
The Richly Dressed Man	Edgar Stehli
The Poorly Dressed Man	Philip Wood
The Old Guard	Walton Butterfield
The Magistrate	Albert Perry
Louise	Evelyn Chard

THE CLOISTER

by EMILE VERHAEREN

Staged by Emanuel Reicher
Settings by Sheldon K. Viele
Garrick Theatre (*Special Performances*), *June 5 and 12, 1921*

Dom Balthazar	Georges Renavent
Father Thomas	Frank Reicher
Dom Militien	Erskine Sanford
Dom Mark	Brandon Peters
Theodule	Edgar Stehli
Idesbald	Henry Travers
Prior	Albert Perry
1st Monk	Philip Wood
2nd Monk	George Frenger
3rd Monk	Walton Butterfield
4th Monk	William Franklin

Fourth Season

AMBUSH

by ARTHUR RICHMAN

*Staged by Robert Milton
Settings by Sheldon K. Viele
Garrick Theatre, Oct. 10, 1921*

Walter Nichols	Frank Reicher
Harriet Nichols	Jane Wheatley
Harry Gleason	Charles Ellis
Margaret Nichols	Florence Eldridge
Seymour Jennison	John Craig
Mrs. Jennison	Catherine Proctor
A Chauffeur	Edwin R. Wolfe
Alan Kraigne	Noel Leslie
Howard Kraigne	Edward Donnelly
George Lithridge	George Stillwell

BOUBOUROCHE

by GEORGE COURTELINE

Produced by Philip Moeller

THE WIFE WITH A SMILE

by DENY AMIEL and ANDRÉ OBEY

Staged by Frank Reicher
Settings by Sheldon K. Viele
Garrick Theatre, Nov. 28, 1921

BOUBOUROCHE

Boubouroche	Arnold Daly
Potasse	Edwin R. Wolfe
An Old Gentleman	Edgar Stehli
Roth	Carl Anderson
Fouettard	Ernest Cossart
Henri	Philip Loeb
Cashier	Katherine Clinton
André	Robert Donaldson
Adèle	Olive May

THE WIFE WITH A SMILE

Mme. Beaudet	Blanche Yurka
Gabrielle	Martha Bryan Allen
M. Beaudet	Arnold Daly
Marguèrite Prévot	Catherine Proctor
Mme. Lebas	Katherine Clinton
M. Lebas	Ernest Cossart
Jacques Dauzat	Edwin R. Wolfe
Eugénie	Jeanne Wainwright
A Clerk	Philip Loeb

HE WHO GETS SLAPPED

by LEONID ANDREIEV

Staged by Robert Milton
Settings and Costumes by Lee Simonson
Garrick Theatre, Jan. 9, 1922

Tilly	Philip Leigh
Polly	Edgar Stehli
Briquet	Ernest Cossart
Mancini	Frank Reicher
Zinida	Helen Westley
Angelica	Martha Bryan Allen
Estelle	Helen Sheridan
François	Edwin R. Wolfe
He	Richard Bennett
Jackson	Henry Travers
Consuelo	Margalo Gillmore
Alfred Bezano	John Rutherford
Baron Regnard	Louis Calvert
A Gentleman	John Blair
Wardrobe Lady	Kathryn Wilson
Usher	Charles Cheltenham
Conductor	Edwin R. Wolfe
Pierre	Philip Loeb
A Sword Dancer	Renee Wilde
Ballet Master	Oliver Grymes
Ballet Girls	Vera Tompkins
	Anne Tonerri
	Marguerite Wernimont
	Frances Ryan

Actresses in Circus Pantomime . . . . Adele St. Maur
Sara Enright
Thomas . . . . Dante Voltaire
A Snake Charmer . . . . Joan Clement
A Contortionist . . . . Richard Coolidge
A Riding Master . . . . Kenneth Lawton
A Juggler . . . . Francis D. Sadtler
Acrobats . . . . Sears Taylor
Luigi Belastro

BACK TO METHUSELAH

by BERNARD SHAW

Staged by
Alice Lewisohn and Agnes Morgan (1st Week)
Frank Reicher (2nd Week)
Philip Moeller (3rd Week)
Settings and Costumes by Lee Simonson
Garrick Theatre, Feb. 27, 1922

First Week of Cycle
PART I

Adam	George Gaul
Eve	Ernita Lascelles
Voice of the Serpent	Margaret Wycherly
Cain	Dennis King

PART II

Franklyn Barnabas	Albert Bruning
Conrad Barnabas	Moffat Johnston
Parlor Maid	Margaret Wycherly
Haslam	Stanley Howlett
Savvy	Eleanor Woodruff
Joyce-Burge	A. P. Kaye
Lubin	Claude King

Second Week of Cycle
PART III

Burge-Lubin, President of the British Isles	A. P. Kaye
Barnabas, the Accountant General	Moffat Johnston
Confucius, the Chief Secretary	Claude King
The Minister of Health	Mary Lawton
The Archbishop of York	Stanley Howlett
Mrs. Lutestring, the Domestic Minister	Margaret Wycherly

PART IV

The Elderly Gentleman	Albert Bruning
The Woman	Ernita Lascelles
Zozim	Claude King
Zoo	Eleanor Woodruff
Napoleon	George Gaul
The Oracle	Margaret Wycherly
The Envoy	A. P. Kaye
The Envoy's Wife	Shirley King
The Envoy's Daughter	Martha-Bryan Allen

Third Week of Cycle
PART V

Strephon	Dennis King
A Maiden	Eleanor Woodruff
The He-Ancient	Moffat Johnston
Acis	Walter Abel
The She-Ancient	Margaret Wycherly
Ecrasia	Catherine Dale Owen
Arjillax	Stanley Howlett
Martellus	Claude King
The Newly-Born	Martha-Bryan Allen
Pygmalion	A. P. Kaye
The Male Figure	George Gaul
The Female Figure	Ernita Lascelles
The Ghost of Adam	George Gaul
The Ghost of Eve	Ernita Lascelles
The Ghost of Cain	Dennis King
The Voice of the Serpent	Margaret Wycherly
Lilith	Mary Lawton

WHAT THE PUBLIC WANTS

by ARNOLD BENNETT

Staged by Louis Calvert
Settings by Sheldon K. Viele
Garrick Theatre, May 1, 1922

Sir Charles Worgan	Charles Dalton
Saul Kendrick	Malcom Dunn
Francis Worgan	Claude King
Page Boy	Francis Sadtler
Simon Macquoid	Stanley Howlett
Emily Vernon	Margaret Wycherly
Holt St. John	Louis Calvert
Mrs. Cleland (**Henrietta Blackwood**)	Jane Wheatley
Samuel Cleland	William A. Evans
Mrs. Downes	Emily Fitzroy
Annie Worgan	Shirley King
John Worgan	Moffat Johnston
Mrs. Worgan	Marietta Hyde
James Brindley	Harry Ashford

FROM MORN TO MIDNIGHT

by Georg Kaiser

Translated by Ashley Dukes
Staged by Frank Reicher
Settings by Lee Simonson
Garrick Theatre, May 21, 1922

Cashier	Frank Reicher
Stout Gentleman	Ernest Cossart
Clerk	Sears Taylor
Messenger Boy	Francis Sadtler
Lady	Helen Westley
Bank Manager	Henry Travers
Muffled Gentleman	Allyn Joslyn
Serving Maid	Adele St. Maur
Porter	Charles Cheltenham
The Lady's Son	Edgar Stehli
The Cashier's Mother	Kathryn Wilson
His Daughters	Lela May Aultman
	Julia Cobb
His Wife	Ernita Lascelles
First Gentleman	Walton Butterfield
Second Gentleman	Philip Leigh
Third Gentleman	Herman Goodman
Fourth Gentleman	Samuel Baron
Fifth Gentleman	William Crowell
Salvation Lass	Helen Sheridan
Waiter	Edgar Stehli
First Mask	Clelia Benjamin
Second Mask	Adele St. Maur

Third Mask	Caroline Hancock
Fourth Mask	Annette Ponse
First Guest	Sears Taylor
Second Guest	Allyn Joslyn
Third Guest	Sam Rosen
Officer of Salvation Army	Ernita Lascelles
First Soldier of Salvation Army	Philip Leigh
First Penitent	Philip Loeb
Second Soldier of Salvation Army	Camille Pastorfield
Second Penitent	Helen Westley
Third Soldier of Salvation Army	Henry Travers
Third Penitent	Ernest Cossart
Fourth Soldier of Salvation Army	William Crowell
Policeman	Herman Goodman

Fifth Season

R. U. R.

by KAREL CAPEK

Adapted by Paul Selver and Nigel Playfair
Staged by Philip Moeller
Settings and Costumes by Lee Simonson
Garrick Theatre, Oct. 9, 1922

Harry Domin	Basil Sydney
Sulla: a Robotess	Mary Bonestell
Marius: a Robot	Myrtland LaVarre
Helena Glory	Kathlene MacDonell
Dr. Gall	William Devereux
Mr. Fabry	John Anthony
Dr. Hallemier	Moffat Johnston
Mr. Alquist	Louis Calvert
Consul Busman	Henry Travers
Nana	Helen Westley
Radius: a Robot	John Rutherford
Helena: a Robotess	Mary Hone
Primus: a Robot	John Roche
A Servant	Frederick Mark
First Robot	Domis Plugge
Second Robot	Richard Coolidge
Third Robot	Bernard Savage

THE LUCKY ONE

by A. A. MILNE

Settings by Lee Simonson
Staged by Komisarshevsky
Garrick Theatre, Nov. 20, 1922

Tommy Todd	Romney Brent
Henry Wentworth	Harry Ashford
Butler	Leonard Perry
Gerald Farringdon	Dennis King
Miss Farringdon	Helen Westley
Letty Herbert	Gwynedd Vernon
Lady Farringdon	Grace Elliston
Sir James Farringdon	Robert Ayrton
Pamela Carey	Violet Heming
Bob Farringdon	Percy Waram
Mason	Nannie Griffen

THE TIDINGS BROUGHT TO MARY

by PAUL CLAUDEL

Translated by Louise Morgan Sill
Staged by Komisarshevsky
Settings and Costumes by Lee Simonson
Garrick Theatre, Dec. 25, 1922

Violaine	Jeanne de Casalis
Pierre de Craon	Charles Francis
Mara	Mary Fowler
The Mother	Helen Westley
Anne Vercors, the Father	Stanley Howlett
Jacques Hury	Percy Waram
The Mayor of Chevroche	Harry Ashford
The Apprentice of Pierre de Craon	Philip Leigh

PEER GYNT

by HENRIK IBSEN (*Archer's translation*)

Staged by Komisarshevsky
Settings and Costumes by Lee Simonson
Garrick Theatre, Feb. 5, 1923

Peer	Joseph Schildkraut
Åse	Louise Closser Hale
Ingrid, the Bride	Bertha Broad
Mads Moen, the Bridegroom	William Franklin
Bridegroom's Mother	Ellen Larned
Bridegroom's Father	Philip Leigh
Aslak, the Smith	Stanley G. Wood
Dancers	Albert Carroll
	Barbara Kitson
Bride's Father	Stanley Howlett
Solveig's Father	William M. Griffith
Solveig's Mother	Elizabeth Zachry
Solveig	Selena Royle
Helga	Francene Wouters
Old Man of Hegstad	C. Porter Hall
Another Old Man	J. Andrew Johnson
Herd Girls	Elise Bartlett
	Eve Casanova
	Helen Sheridan
The Troll King's Daughter	Helen Westley
The Troll King	Dudley Digges
The Troll Chamberlain	William Franklin
Troll Courtiers	Philip Leigh
	Stanley G. Wood
	William M. Griffith

The Ugly Brat	Francene Wouters
Kari, a Farmer's Wife	Armina Marshall
Trumpeterstrale	Philip Leigh
Mr. Cotton	Stanley G. Wood
Monsieur Ballon	Albert Carroll
Von Eberkopf	Edward G. Robinson
Thief	Romney Brent
Receiver	Alfred Alexandre
Officer	Charles Tazewell
Anitra	Lillebil Ibsen
Begriffenfeldt	Charles Halton
1st Keeper	C. Porter Hall
2nd Keeper	J. Andrew Johnson
Fellah	William Franklin
Hussein	Stanley Howlett
The Button-Moulder	Edward G. Robinson

THE ADDING MACHINE

by ELMER RICE

Staged by Philip Moeller
Settings by Lee Simonson
Garrick Theatre, March 18, 1923

Mr. Zero	Dudley Digges
Mrs. Zero	Helen Westley
Daisy Diana Dorothea Devore	Margaret Wycherly
The Boss	Irving Dillon
Mr. One	Harry McKenna
Mrs. One	Marcia Harris
Mr. Two	Paul Hayes
Mrs. Two	Theresa Stewart
Mr. Three	Gerald Lundegard
Mrs. Three	Georgiana Wilson
Mr. Four	George Stehli
Mrs. Four	Edith Burnett
Mr. Five	William W. Griffith
Mrs. Five	Ruby Craven
Mr. Six	Daniel Hamilton
Mrs. Six	Louise Sydmeth
Policemen	Irving Dillon
	Lewis Barrington
Judy O'Grady	Elise Bartlett
Young Man	Gerald Lundegard
Shrdlu	Edgar G. Robinson
A Head	Daniel Hamilton
Lieutenant Charles	Louis Calvert
Joe	William W. Griffith

THE DEVIL'S DISCIPLE

by BERNARD SHAW

Staged by Philip Moeller
Settings by Lee Simonson
Costumes by Carolyn Hancock
Garrick Theatre, April 23, 1923

Mrs. Annie Primrose Dudgeon	Helen Westley
Essie	Martha-Bryan Allen
Christy	Gerald Hamer
Anthony Anderson	Moffat Johnston
Judith Anderson	Lotus Robb
Lawyer Hawkins	Alan MacAteer
William Dudgeon	Byron Russell
Mrs. William Dudgeon	Katheryn Wilson
Titus Dudgeon	Lawrence Cecil
Mrs. Titus Dudgeon	Maud Ainslie
Richard Dudgeon	Basil Sydney
The Sergeant	Lawrence Cecil
Major Swindon	Reginald Goode
General Burgoyne	Roland Young
Mr. Brudenell	Byron Russell

Sixth Season

WINDOWS

by JOHN GALSWORTHY

*Staged by Moffat Johnston
Settings by Carolyn Hancock
Garrick Theatre, Oct. 8, 1923*

Mary March	Frieda Inescort
Johnny March	Kenneth MacKenna
Geoffrey March	Moffat Johnston
Mrs. March	Helen Westley
Mr. Bly	Henry Travers
Cook	Alice Belmore
Faith Bly	Phyllis Povah
Blunter	George Baxter
Mr. Barnabas	Frank Tweed

THE FAILURES ("LES RATÉS")

by H. R. LENORMAND

Staged by Stark Young
Settings by Lee Simonson
Garrick Theatre, Nov. 19, 1923

Montredon	Dudley Digges
He	Jacob Ben Ami
She	Winifred Lenihan
Second Phantom	Sterling Halloway
The Musician	Erskine Sanford
The Bell Boy	Philip Loeb
Larnaudy	Henry Crosby
A Dresser	Helen Westley
The Ingenue	Helen Tilden
The Duenna	Alice Belmore Cliffe
An Actor	Ernest A. Daniels
Saint-Gallet	Henry Travers
The Magistrate	Morris Carnovsky
Magistrate's Daughter	Hildegarde Halliday
The Private	Ernest A. Daniels
The Corporal	Jo Mielziner
The Librarian	Philip Loeb
His Wife	Ida Zeitlin
The Rake	Herbert Ashton
The Chemist	Henry Clement
The Barmaid	Yvonne Sec
A Hunchback Girl	Polly Craig
A Commissioner of Police	Morris Carnovsky

THE RACE WITH THE SHADOW

by WILHELM VON SCHOLZ

Staged by Philip Moeller
Settings by Carolyn Hancock
Garrick Theatre (matinees only), Dec. 14, 1923

Dr. Hans Martin, a Writer	Arnold Daly
Margaret, his Wife	Helen Westley
A Stranger	Jacob Ben Ami
Maid	Armina Marshall

SAINT JOAN

by BERNARD SHAW

Staged by Philip Moeller
Settings and Costumes by Raymond Sovey
Garrick Theatre, Dec. 28, 1923

Robert de Baudricourt	Ernest Cossart
Steward	William M. Griffith
Joan	Winifred Lenihan
Bertrand de Poulengy	Frank Tweed
The Archbishop of Rheims	Albert Bruning
La Tremouille, Constable of France	Herbert Ashton
Court Page	Jo Mielziner
Gilles de Rais, Bluebeard	Walton Butterfield
Captain la Hire	Morris Carnovsky
The Dauphin, (later Charles VII)	Philip Leigh
Duchess de la Tremouille	Elizabeth Pearré
Dunois, Bastard of Orleans	Maurice Colbourne
Dunois' Page	James Norris
Richard de Beauchamp, Earl of Warwick	A. H. Van Buren
Chaplain de Stogumber	Henry Travers
Peter Cauchon, Bishop of Beauvais	Ian Maclaren
Warwick's Page	Seth Baldwin
The Inquisitor	Joseph Macaulay
Canon D'Estivet	Philip Wood
De Courcelles, Canon of Paris	Walton Butterfield
Brother Martin Ladvenu	Morris Carnovsky
The Executioner	Herbert Ashton
An English Soldier	Frank Tweed
A Gentleman of 1920	Ernest Cossart

FATA MORGANA

by Ernest Vadja

Translated by James L. A. Burrell
Staged by Philip Moeller
Settings and Costumes by Lee Simonson
Garrick Theatre, March 3, 1924

George	Morgan Farley
His Mother	Josephine Hull
Annie, his Sister	Patricia Barclay
His Father	William Ingersoll
Peter	James Jolley
Rosalie	Helen Westley
Blazy	Charles Cheltenham
Mrs. Blazy	Armina Marshall
Therese	Julia Cobb
Katherine	Edith Meiser
Henry	Sterling Holloway
Franciska	Barbara Wilson
Charley Blazy	Paul E. Martin
Mathilde Fay	Emily Stevens
Gabriel Fay	Orlando Daly

MAN AND THE MASSES ("MASSE MENSCH")

by ERNST TOLLER

Translated by Louis Untermeyer
Staged and designed by Lee Simonson
Garrick Theatre, April 14, 1924

The Woman	Blanche Yurka
The Man, her Husband	Ullrich Haupt
The Nameless One	Jacob Ben Ami
(*The Spirit of the Masses*)	
The Companion (*a dream figure*)	Arthur Hughes
First Banker	A. P. Kaye
Second Banker	William Franklin
Third Banker	Erskine Sanford
Fourth Banker	Leonard Loan
Fifth Banker	Barry Jones
Sixth Banker	Charles Tazewell
The Condemned One	John McGovern
First Working Man	Maurice McRae
Second Working Man	Allyn Joslyn
Third Working Man	Marling Chilton
Fourth Working Man	Samuel Rosen
Fifth Working Man	Robert Brodeur
A Working Woman	Pauline Moore
An Officer	Charles Tazewell
A Priest	Erskine Sanford
First Woman Prisoner	Zita Johann
Second Woman Prisoner	Mariette Hyde
Messenger Boy	Sidney Dexter

Seventh Season

THE GUARDSMAN

by FERENC MOLNAR

*Staged by Philip Moeller
Settings by Jo Mielziner
Garrick Theatre, Oct. 13, 1924*

The Actor	Alfred Lunt
The Actress, his Wife	Lynn Fontanne
The Critic	Dudley Digges
"Mamma"	Helen Westley
Liesel	Edith Meiser
A Creditor	Philip Loeb
An Usher	Kathryn Wilson

THEY KNEW WHAT THEY WANTED

by SIDNEY HOWARD

Staged by Philip Moeller
Settings by Carolyn Hancock
Garrick Theatre, Nov. 24, 1924

Joe	Glenn Anders
Father McKee	Charles Kennedy
Ah Gee	Allen Atwell
Tony	Richard Bennett
The R. F. D.	Robert Cook
Amy	Pauline Lord
Angelo	Hardwick Nevin
Giorgio	Jacob Zollinger
The Doctor	Charles Tazewell
First Italian Mother	Frances Hyde
Her Daughter	Antoinette Bizzoco
Second Mother	Peggy Conway
Her Son	Edward Rosenfeld

PROCESSIONAL

by John Howard Lawson

Staged by Philip Moeller
Settings by Mordekai Gorelik
Garrick Theatre, Jan. 12, 1925

Boob Elkins, a Newsboy	Ben Grauer
Isaac Cohen, who keeps the General Store	Philip Loeb
Sadie Cohen, his Daughter	June Walker
Jake Psinski	Charles Halton
Pop Pratt, a Civil War Veteran	William T. Hays
MacCarthy } *Soldiers*	Carl Eckstrom
Bill	Alan Ward
Phillpots, a Newspaper Man	Donald Macdonald
The Sheriff	Redfield Clarke
A Man in a Silk Hat	Horace M. Gardner
Old Maggie	Patricia Barclay
Mrs. Euphemia Stewart Flimmins	Blanche Friderici
Dynamite Jim	George Abbott
Rastus	Samuel L. Manning
Slop	Robert Collyer
Smith	Stanley Lindahl
1st Soldier	Lee Strasberg
2nd Soldier	Stanley Lindahl
3rd Soldier	Roy Requa
4th Soldier	Samuel Chinitz

ARIADNE

by A. A. Milne

Staged by Philip Moeller
Settings by Carolyn Hancock
Garrick Theatre, Feb. 23, 1925

Ariadne Winter	Laura Hope Crews
John Winter, her Husband	Lee Baker
Mary	Armina Marshall
Hector Chadwick	Orlando Daly
Hestor Chadwick	Catherine Proctor
Janet Ingleby	Frieda Inescort
Horace Meldrum	Harry Mestayer

CAESAR AND CLEOPATRA

by BERNARD SHAW

Staged by Philip Moeller
Settings by Frederick Jones III
Costumes by Aline Bernstein
Guild Theatre, April 13, 1925

Belzanor	Lawrence Cecil
The Persian	Francis Verdi
Sentinel	Maurice McRae
Nubian Sentinel	Harold Harding
Bel Affris	George Baxter
A Woman	Mary Tupper
Ftatateeta	Helen Westley
Caesar	Lionel Atwill
Cleopatra	Helen Hayes
Slave	Rupert Bannister
Three Women Slaves	Sylvia Shear
	Hildegarde Halliday
	Marion Hahn
Rufio	Edmund Elton
Chamberlain	Leete Stone
Achillas	Maurice McRae
Ptolemy	Teddy Jones
Pothinus	Albert Bruning
Theodotus	Maurice Cass
Britannus	Henry Travers
Lucius Septimus	George Baxter
Wounded Roman Soldier	Edwin A. Brown
Roman Sentinel	Jack Trevor

Apollodorus	Schuyler Ladd
Four Market Porters	James Norris
	Harold Clurman
	James W. Wallace
	Felix Jacoves
Centurion	Maurice McRae
First Auxiliary Soldier	Edwin A. Brown
Second Auxiliary Soldier	Lewis McMichael
Boatman	Starr Jones
Musician	Leonard Loan
Iris	Hildegarde Halliday
Charmian	Joan Marion
Palace Official	Charles Cheltenham
Major Domo	Lawrence Cecil
A Priest	James W. Wallace

ARMS AND THE MAN

by Bernard Shaw

Staged by Philip Moeller
Settings and Costumes by Lee Simonson
Guild Theatre, Sept. 14, 1925

Raina	Lynn Fontanne
Catherine	Jane Wheatley
Louka	Stella Larrimore
Captain Bluntschli	Alfred Lunt
Russian Officer	Maurice McRae
Major Petkoff	Ernest Cossart
Nicola	Henry Travers
Sergius	Pedro de Cordoba

Eighth Season

THE GLASS SLIPPER

by Ferenc Molnar

Staged by Philip Moeller
Settings by Lee Simonson
Guild Theatre, Oct. 19, 1925

Irma Szabo	June Walker
Lilly	Eddie Wragge
Adele Romajzer	Helen Westley
Kati	Armina Marshall
Paul Csaszar	George Baxter
Lajos Sipos	Lee Baker
Adele's Mother	Veni Atherton
Cook	Elizabeth Pendleton
Janitor	Stanley G. Wood
Julcsa	Ethel Westley
Photographer	John McGovern
Assistant Photographer	Roland Hoot
Viola	Evelyn Bareed
Stetner	Martin Wolfson
Bandi Sasz	Louis Cruger
Captail Gal	Erskine Sanford
Gypsy Leader	Ralph MacBane
Police Clerk	Martin Wolfson
Police Sergeant	Erskine Sanford
Policeman	Milton Salsbury
Mrs. Rotics	Amelia Summerville
Mrs. Rotics' Companion	Jeanne La Gue
Ilona Keczeli	Ethel Valentine
Dr. Theodore Sagody	Ralph MacBane
Sergeant-at-Arms	Louis Cruger
Police Magistrate	Edward Fielding

THE MAN OF DESTINY
ANDROCLES AND THE LION

by BERNARD SHAW

Staged by Philip Moeller
Klaw Theatre, Nov. 23, 1925

THE MAN OF DESTINY
Settings by Carolyn Hancock

Napoleon	Tom Powers
Giuseppi	Edward G. Robinson
Lieutenant	Reginald Owen
The Lady	Clare Eames

ANDROCLES AND THE LION
Settings by Miguel Covarrubias

The Lion	Romney Brent
Androcles	Henry Travers
Megaera	Alice Cliff
Beggar	Richard Nye
Centurion	Reginald Owen
Captain	Tom Powers
Lavinia	Clare Eames
Lentullus	Romney Brent
Metellus	Allan Ward
Spintho	Philip Leigh
Ferrvius	Orville Caldwell
Ox Driver	Samuel Rosen
Retiarius	William Griffith
Secutor	Frederick Chilton
Call Boy	Alfred Little
Keeper	Lloyd Neal
Caesar	Edward G. Robinson

MERCHANTS OF GLORY

by Marcel Pagnol and Paul Nivoix

Translated by Ralph Roeder
Staged by Philip Moeller
Settings by Ben Webster
Guild Theatre, Dec. 14, 1925

Madame Bachelet	Helen Westley
Yvonne	Betty Linley
Germaine Bachelet	Armina Marshall
Grandel	Lee Baker
Bachelet	Augustin Duncan
Pigal	George Nash
A Man	Philip Loeb
Lieutenant-Colonel Blancard	Lowden Adams
Richebon	Charles Halton
Monsieur Denis	Jose Ruben
Comte de l'Eauville	Edward Fielding
Secretary	Stanley G. Wood
Usher	Philip Loeb

GOAT SONG

by Franz Werfel

Translated by Ruth Langner
Staged by Jacob Ben-Ami
Settings and Costumes by Lee Simonson
Guild Theatre, Jan 25, 1926

Gospodar Stevan Milic	George Gaul
Gospodar Jevrem Vesilic	Henry Travers
Mirko's Mother	Blanche Yurka
Stanja's Mother	Judith Lowry
Stanja	Lynn Fontanne
Mirko	Dwight Frye
Babka	Helen Westley
A Maid	Lorna McLean
Young Serving Man	Philip Loeb
Physician	Albert Bruning
Messenger	Bela Blau
Starzina	Erskine Sanford
Elder of Krasnokraj	Stanley G. Wood
Elder of Modrygor	Philip Loeb
Elder of Medegya	Anthony André
Clerk	Harold Clurman
The American	Edward Fielding
Teiterlik	Herbert Yost
Reb Feiwel	Edward G. Robinson
Bogoboj, the Peasant Prophet	William Ingersoll
Kruna	Zita Johann
Juvan	Alfred Lunt
An Old Man	Anthony André
Innkeeper	Martin Wolfson
Priest	Erskine Sanford
Bashi Bazook	House Baker Jameson
Scavenger	Henry Travers

THE CHIEF THING

by Nicolas Evreinoff

Staged by Philip Moeller and the Author
Settings and Costumes by Sergei Soudeikine
Guild Theatre, March 22, 1926

Paraklete	McKay Morris
Lady with the Dog	Edith Meiser
Retired Government Clerk	Henry Travers
A Dancer	Estelle Winwood
An Actor, who plays the Lover	C. Stafford Dickens
Landlady in Rooming House	Alice Belmore Cliffe
Her Daughter, a Stenographer	Esther Mitchell
A Student	Dwight Frye
The Manager of a Provincial Theatre	Stanley G. Wood
A Stage Director	Edward G. Robinson
Electrician	William Griffith
Nero	Harold Clurman
Petronius	Romney Brent
Tigelin	Donald Angus
Lucian	House Baker Jameson
Popea Sabina	Peggy Conway
Ligia	Kate Lawson
Cavlia Crispinilla } *Actors in a Provincial Theatre* {	Mary True
Nigidia	Hildegarde Halliday
A Prompter	Lee Strasberg
A Slave	Willard Tobias
A Comedian	Ernest Cossart
A School Teacher	Helen Westley
A Fallen Woman	Patricia Barron
A Deaf Mute	Hildegarde Halliday

AT MRS. BEAM'S

by C. K. MUNRO

Staged by Philip Moeller
Settings by Carolyn Hancock
Guild Theatre, April 26, 1926

Miss Shoe	Jean Cadell
Mr. Durrows	Henry Travers
Miss Cheezle	Helen Strickland
Mrs. Bebb	Helen Westley
James Bebb	Paul Nugent
Mrs. Stone	Phyllis Connard
Miss Newman	Dorothy Fletcher
Mrs. Beam	Daisy Belmore
Mr. Dermott	Alfred Lunt
Laura Pasquale	Lynn Fontanne
Colin Langford	Leslie Barrie

Ninth Season

JUAREZ AND MAXIMILIAN
by Franz Werfel

Staged by Philip Moeller
Settings and Costumes by Lee Simonson
Guild Theatre, Oct. 11, 1926

Clarke, War Correspondent for the N. Y. Herald	Stanley DeWolfe
Elizea, Secretary to President Juarez	Philip Loeb
City Deputy of Chihuahua	Philip Leigh
Mariano Escobedo	Harold Clurman
Porfirio Diaz	Edward G. Robinson
Riva-Palacio	Morris Carnovsky
Maximilian, Archduke of Austria, now Emperor of Mexico	Alfred Lunt
Captain Miguel Lopez	Edward Van Sloan
Doctor Basch	Albert Bruning
Grill (Servant)	John Rynne
Madame Barrio, Lady-in-Waiting	Cheryl Crawford
State Councillor Stephen Herzfield	Earle Larimore
Empress Charlotte	Clare Eames
Archbishop Labastida	Dudley Digges
Theodosio Lares	Edward Hogan
Lawyer Siliceo	Erskine Sanford
General Tomas Mejia	Philip Loeb
François Achille Bazaine, Marshal of France	Arnold Daly
Edouard Pierron, Aide to Bazaine	Maurice McRae
Iturbide	Freddie Stange
Blasio, the Private Secretary to the Emperor	Sanford Meisner
General Marquez	Dan Walker

General Miramon	Felix Jacoves
Corporal Wimberger	Stanley DeWolfe
Yapitan	Philip Leigh
Polyphemio	Harold Clurman
Princess Agnes Salm	Margalo Gillmore
José Rincon Gallardo	Erskine Sanford
Official	Roland Twombley
Canon Soria	Morris Carnovsky

PYGMALION

by BERNARD SHAW

Staged by Dudley Digges
Settings by Jo Mielziner
Guild Theatre, Nov. 15, 1926

Clara Hill, the Daughter	Phyllis Connard
Mrs. Eynsford Hill, the Mother	Winifred Hanley
A Bystander	Charles Cardon
Freddy Hill, the Son	Charles Courtniedge
Eliza Doolittle, the Flower-girl	Lynn Fontanne
Colonel Pickering, the Gentleman	J. W. Austin
Another Bystander	Bernard Savage
The Sarcastic Bystander	Leigh Lovel
An Elderly Gentleman	Thomas Meegan
An Elderly Lady	Kitty Wilson
Henry Higgins, the Notetaker	Reginald Mason
Taxi Driver	Edward Hartford
Mrs. Pearce	Beryl Mercer
Alfred Doolittle	Henry Travers
Mrs. Higgins	Helen Westley
The Maid	Dorothy Fletcher

NED McCOBB'S DAUGHTER

by SIDNEY HOWARD

Staged by Philip Moeller
Settings by Aline Bernstein
John Golden Theatre, Nov. 22, 1926

Carrie Callahan	Clare Eames
First Federal Man	Maurice McRae
Nat Glidden	Philip Loeb
Second Federal Man	Morris Carnovsky
Jenny	Margalo Gillmore
Babe Callahan	Alfred Lunt
Captain Ned McCobb	Dudley Digges
George Callahan	Earle Larimore
Lawyer Grover	Edward G. Robinson
Ben McCobb	Philip Leigh

THE SILVER CORD

by SIDNEY HOWARD

Staged by John Cromwell
Settings by Kate D. Lawson
John Golden Theatre, Dec. 20, 1926

Hester	Margalo Gillmore
David	Elliot Cabot
Christina	Elizabeth Risdon
Robert	Earle Larimore
Mrs. Phelps	Laura Hope Crews
Maid	Barbara Bruce

THE BROTHERS KARAMAZOV

Dramatization by JACQUES COPEAU

Staged by Jacques Copeau
Settings by Raymond Sovey
Guild Theatre, Jan. 3, 1927

Aliocha Feodorovitch Karamazov, *Feodor's Youngest Son*	Morris Carnovsky
Dmitri Feodorovitch Karamazov, *Feodor's Eldest Son*	Alfred Lunt
Smerdiakov	Edward G. Robinson
Ivan Feodorovitch Karamazov, *Feodor's Second Son*	George Gaul
Feodor Pavlovitch Karamazov	Dudley Digges
Father Zossima	Philip Leigh
Katerina Ivanovna Verhovovtseva	Clare Eames
Agrafena Alexandrovna Svetlov (Grouchenka)	Lynn Fontanne
A Maid	Dorothy Fletcher
Grigori Vassilievitch	Henry Travers
Lieutenant Moussialovitch	Herbert Ashton
Vroubleski, his Friend	Philip Loeb
Trifon Borisitch, an Innkeeper	Charles Carden
Andrey, a Coachman	Charles Courtniedge
Arina	Phyllis Connard
Stepanida	Dorothy Fletcher
Chief of Police	Bernard Savage

RIGHT YOU ARE IF YOU THINK YOU ARE

by Pirandello

Staged by Philip Moeller
Settings by Jo Mielziner
Guild Theatre, March 2, 1927

Lamberto Laudisi	Reginald Mason
Signora Frola	Beryl Mercer
Ponza	Edward G. Robinson
Signora Ponza	Armina Marshall
Commendatore	Morris Carnovsky
Amalia	Laura Hope Crews
Dina	Phyllis Connard
Sirelli	Henry Travers
Signora Sirelli	Elizabeth Risdon
Prefect	J. W. Austin
Centuri	Philip Loeb
Signora Cini	Helen Westley
Signora Nenni	Dorothy Fletcher
Butler	Maurice McRae
A Gentleman	Philip Leigh

THE SECOND MAN

by S. N. BEHRMAN

Staged by Philip Moeller
Settings by Jo Mielziner
Guild Theatre, April 11, 1927

Mrs. Kendall Frayne	Lynn Fontanne
Clark Storey	Alfred Lunt
Austin Lowe	Earle Larimore
Monica Grey	Margalo Gillmore
Albert	Edward Hartford

Tenth Season

PORGY

by Dorothy and Du Bose Heyward

Staged by Rouben Mamoulian
Settings by Cleon Throckmorton
Guild Theatre, Oct. 11, 1927

Maria, Keeper of the Cookshop	Georgette Harvey
Jake, Captain of the Fishing Fleet	Wesley Hill
Lily	Dorothy Paul
Mingo	Richard Huey
Annie	Ella Madison
Sporting Life	Percy Verwayne
Serena, Robbins' Wife	Rose MacClendon
Robbins, a Young Stevedore	Lloyd Gray
Jim, a Stevedore	Peter Clark
Clara, Jake's Wife	Marie Young
Peter, the Honeyman	Hayes Pryor
Porgy, a Crippled Beggar	Frank Wilson
Crown, a Stevedore	Jack Carter
Crown's Bess	Evelyn Ellis
A Detective	Stanley DeWolfe
Two Policemen	Hugh Rennie
	Maurice McRae
Undertaker	Leigh Whipper
Scipio	Melville Greene
Simon Frazier, a Lawyer	A. B. Comathiere
Nelson, a Fisherman	G. Edward Brown
Alan Archdale	Edward Fielding
The Crab Man	Leigh Whipper
The Coroner	Garrett Minturn

THE DOCTOR'S DILEMMA

by BERNARD SHAW

Staged by Dudley Digges
Settings by Jo Mielziner
Guild Theatre, Nov. 21, 1927
(Produced first in Chicago)

Redpenny	Charles Romano
Emmy	Helen Westley
Sir Colenso Ridgeon	Baliol Holloway
Dr. Schutzmacher	Morris Carnovsky
Sir Patrick Cullen	Dudley Digges
Mr. Cutler Walpole	Earle Larimore
Sir Ralph Bloomfield Bonington	Ernest Cossart
Dr. Blenkinsop	Henry Travers
Jennifer Dubedat	Lynn Fontanne
Louis Dubedat	Alfred Lunt
Minnie Tinwell	Phyllis Connard
Newspaper Man	Philip Leigh
Secretary	Charles Romano
A Waiter	Edward Hartford

MARCO MILLIONS

by Eugene O'Neill

Staged by Rouben Mamoulian
Settings and Costumes by Lee Simonson
Guild Theatre, Jan. 9, 1928

Christian Traveller	Philip Leigh
Magian Traveller	Mark Schweid
Buddhist Traveller	Charles Romano
A Mahometan Captain of Ghazan's Army	Robert Barrat
A Corporal	Albert Van Dekker
Princess Kukachin, Granddaughter of Kublai	Margalo Gillmore
Marco Polo	Alfred Lunt
Donata	Natalie Browning
Tedaldo, Papal Legate to Acre	Morris Carnovsky
Nicolo, Marco's Father	Henry Travers
Maffeo, Marco's Uncle	Ernest Cossart
A Dominican Monk	Albert Van Dekker
A Knight Crusader	George Cotton
A Papal Courier	Sanford Meisner
One Ali Brother	H. H. McCollum
Older Ali Brother	Mark Schweid
The Prostitute	Mary Blair
A Dervish	John Henry
An Indian Snake Charmer	John Henry
A Buddhist Priest	Philip Leigh
Emissary from Kublai	Albert Van Dekker
Kublai, the Great Kaan	Baliol Holloway
Chu-Yin, a Cathayan Sage	Dudley Digges
Boatswain	H. H. McCollum

Ghazan, Kaan of Persia	Morris Carnovsky
General Bayan	Robert Barrat
Messenger from Persia	Charles Romano
Paulo Loredano, Donata's Father	John C. Davis
A Buddhist Priest	Charles Romano
A Taoist Priest	Louis Veda
A Confucian Priest	Mark Schweid
A Moslem Priest	H. H. McCollum

STRANGE INTERLUDE

by Eugene O'Neill

Staged by Philip Moeller
Settings by Jo Mielziner
John Golden Theatre, Jan. 23, 1928
(This play ran for 432 consecutive performances in New York, the Guild record.)

Charles Marsden	Tom Powers
Professor Leeds	Philip Leigh
Nina Leeds	Lynn Fontanne
Sam Evans	Earle Larimore
Edmund Darrell	Glenn Anders
Mrs. Amos Evans	Helen Westley
Gordon Evans, as a Boy	Charles Walters
Madeline Arnold	Ethel Westley
Gordon Evans, as a Man	John J. Burns

VOLPONE

by Stephan Zweig

Adapted from Ben Jonson
Translated by Ruth Langner
Staged by Philip Moeller
Settings and Costumes by Lee Simonson
Guild Theatre, April 9, 1928

First Singer	Lucian Tranto
Second Singer	Vincent Sherman
Third Singer	William Edmonson
Fourth Singer	George Ballard
First Groom	Louis Veda
Second Groom	Mark Schweid
Mosca (the Gadfly)	Alfred Lunt
Volpone (the Fox)	Dudley Digges
Slave to Volpone	John Henry
Voltore (the Vulture)	Philip Leigh
Corvino (the Crow)	Ernest Cossart
Corbaccio (the Raven)	Henry Travers
Canina (the Bitch)	Helen Westley
Colomba, Wife of Corvino (the Dove)	Margalo Gillmore
Maid to Colomba	Mary Bell
Corbaccio's Servant	John C. Davis
Leone, Captain of the Fleet (the Lion)	McKay Morris
Captain of the Sbirri	Albert Van Dekker
Judge	Morris Carnovsky
Clerk of the Court	Sanford Meisner
Court Attendants	Leonard Perry
	Vincent Sherman
Priest	John C. Davis

Eleventh Season

FAUST, PART I

English version by Graham *and* Tristan Rawson

Staged by Friedrich Holl
Settings and Costumes by Lee Simonson
Guild Theatre, Oct. 8, 1928

Raphael	Martin Wolfson
Gabriel	Douglass Montgomery
Michael	Edward Hogan
The Voice	Maurice Cass
Mephistopheles	Dudley Digges
Faust	George Gaul
Wagner	Walter Vonnegut
Voice of the Earth Spirit	Martin Wolfson
A Young Peasant	Edward Hogan
An Old Peasant	William T. Hays
A Student	William Challee
Siebel	Stanley G. Wood
Frosch	Edward Hogan
Brander	Martin Wolfson
Altmeyer	Herbert J. Biberman
She-Ape	Christine Putnam
He-Ape	Eric Linden
The Witch	Gale Sondergaard
Margaret	Helen Chandler
Martha	Helen Westley
Elizabeth	Anna Kostant
Valentine	Douglass Montgomery
Voice of the Ignis Fatuus	Rita Vale
Lilith	Rita Vale

MAJOR BARBARA

by BERNARD SHAW

Staged by Philip Moeller
Settings by Redington Sharpe
Guild Theatre, Nov. 20, 1928

Stephen Undershaft	Maurice Wells
Lady Britomart Undershaft	Helen Westley
Morrison	Isidore Marcil
Barbara Undershaft	Winifred Lenihan
Sarah Undershaft	Gale Sondergaard
Adolphus Cusins	Elliot Cabot
Charles Lomax	Charles Courtneidge
Andrew Undershaft	Dudley Digges
Rummy Mitchens	Alice Cooper Cliffe
Snobby Price	Edgar Kent
Jenny	Phyllis Connard
Peter Shirley	A. P. Kaye
Bill Walker	Percy Waram
Mrs. Baines	Edythe Tressider
Bilton	Ralph Sumpter

WINGS OVER EUROPE

by Robert Nichols and Maurice Browne

Staged by Rouben Mamoulian
Settings by Raymond Sovey
Martin Beck Theatre, Dec. 10, 1928

Members of the Cabinet Committee:

Walter Grantley, Prime Minister	Ernest Lawford
Lord Sunningdale, Lord Privy Seal	John Dunn
Lord Dedham, Lord High Chancellor	Frank Elliott
Matthew Grindle, Chancellor of the Exchequer	Joseph Kilgour
Sir Humphrey Haliburton, Secretary of State for Home Affairs	Nicholas Joy
Evelyn Arthur, Secretary of State for Foreign Affairs	Frank Conroy
Richard Stapp, Secretary of State for War	Hugh Buckler
Lord Cossington, Secretary of State for The Dominions	Thomas A. Braidon
Esme Falkiner, Secretary of State for the Air	Charles Francis
Sir Romilly Blount, First Lord of the Admiralty	Grant Stewart
Lord Vivian Vere, President of the Board of Education	Robert Rendel
St. John Pascoe, Attorney General	George Graham
H. G. Dunne, First Commissioner of Works	Gordon Richards
Francis Lightfoot	Alexander Kirkland
Sir Berkeley Rummel	Edward Lester
Sir Henry Hand	A. P. Kaye
Hart-Plimsoll	Wheeler Dryden
Taggert	Charles Cardon
Two Cabinet Messengers	Lionel Bevans and Walter Scott

CAPRICE

by SIL-VARA

Adapted and Staged by Philip Moeller
Settings by Aline Bernstein
Hollis St. Theatre, Boston, Dec. 17, 1928
Guild Theatre, Dec. 31, 1928

Von Echardt	Alfred Lunt
A Delicate Lady	Geneva Harrison
Minna	Caroline Newcomb
The Doctor	Ernest Cossart
Clerk	Leonard Loan
Amalia	Lily Cahill
Ilsa Von Ilsen	Lynn Fontanne
Robert	Douglass Montgomery

DYNAMO

by Eugene O'Neill

Staged by Philip Moeller
Settings by Lee Simonson
Martin Beck Theatre, Feb. 11, 1929

Hutchins Light	George Gaul
Amelia Light	Helen Westley
Reuben Light	Glenn Anders
Ramsay Fife	Dudley Digges
May Fife	Catherine Calhoun-Doucet
Ada Fife	Claudette Colbert
Jennings	Ross Forrester
Rocco	Edgar Kent

MAN'S ESTATE

by Beatrice Blackmar and Bruce Gould

Staged by Dudley Digges
Settings by Cleon Throckmorton
Biltmore Theatre, April 1, 1929

Joseph Jordan, Jerry's Uncle	Edward Favor
William P. Jordan, the Father	Dudley Digges
Caroline Jordan, Jerry's Aunt	Florence Gerald
Minnie Jordan, the Mother	Elizabeth Patterson
Jerry Jordan, the Son	Earle Larimore
Emily Bender, their Daughter	Armina Marshall
Dr. Frank Bender, their Son-in-Law	Edward Pawley
Sesaly Blaine, a Guest	Margalo Gillmore
Rev. Dr. Eustace Potter	Louis Veda
Cousin Grace	Maria Ziccardi

THE CAMEL THROUGH THE NEEDLE'S EYE

by FRANTISEK LANGER

Adapted and Staged by Philip Moeller
Settings by Lee Simonson
Martin Beck Theatre, April 15, 1929

Mrs. Pesta	Helen Westley
Pesta	Henry Travers
Street Urchin	Norman Williams
Susi	Miriam Hopkins
Counselor Andrejs	Joseph Kilgour
Director Bezchyba	Morris Carnovsky
Marta Bojok	Catherine Calhoun-Doucet
Alik Vilim	Elliot Cabot
Servant	Percy Waram
Lilli Bojok	Mary Kennedy
Joseph Vilim	Claude Rains
A Medical Student	George Freedley
Servant Girl	Rose Burdick